STRAWBERRY FIELDS

This new play by the author of *Hitting Town* and *City Sugar* is the first National Theatre production to be staged in the Cottlesloe, the National's studio theatre. *Strawberry Fields* is a funny, haunting, frightening play about three young members of the 'lost generation' of the sixties, steeped in folk-memories of open-air pop festivals like Glastonbury and Easy Rider-type road movies. As they journey the length of England in the heat of a summer's day, their apparently harmless jaunt begins to take on increasingly disturbing overtones . . .

STEPHEN POLIAKOFF wrote *Strawberry Fields* while Writer in Residence at the National Theatre.

STRAWBERRY FIELDS

STEPHEN POLIAKOFF

A Methuen New Theatrescript
Eyre Methuen · London

First published in 1977 by Eyre Methuen Ltd, 11 New Fetter Lane,
London EC4P 4EE
Reprinted 1980
Copyright © 1977 by Stephen Poliakoff
Printed in Great Britain by Expression Printers Ltd, London

ISBN 0 413 38470 5

CAUTION
All rights whatsoever in this play are strictly reserved and application for performance
etc. should be made to Margaret Ramsay Ltd, 14a Goodwin's Court, London WC2.
No performance may be given unless a licence has been obtained.

Strawberry Fields was first staged by the National Theatre in the Cottesloe on 1 March 1977. The cast was as follows:

KEVIN	Stephen Rea
CHARLOTTE	Jane Asher
NICK	Kenneth Cranham
MRS ROBERTS	Anne Leon
TAYLOR	Frederick Warder
CLEANER	Maya Kemp
KID	Peter Hugo

Directed by Michael Apted
Designed by Di Seymour

The play is set in various locations up a motorway.

The time is the present.

ACT ONE
Scene One

Cafe, hot, dusty, edge of London, start of the motorway.
CHARLOTTE sitting at a table. Jukebox in the background playing. She is 21. She is drinking orange juice. KEVIN, tall, lanky, with long hair and dark glasses, stands watching her. He is 30. He moves closer as she drinks delicately through a straw. He takes out his wallet, slight smile. He takes out of the wallet a small green card, he puts it on the table and pushes it towards her. CHARLOTTE looks up, she picks up the card, glances back, hands its back. He puts it back in the wallet. She smiles at him. KEVIN sits down at the table glancing over his shoulder as he does so.

KEVIN: I'm Kevin.

CHARLOTTE (*shy smile*): Yes.

KEVIN (*smiles*): Kevin.

Pause.

That's my real name as it happens.

CHARLOTTE: I know.

KEVIN: Good. (*Pause.*) Great then.

CHARLOTTE: And I'm Charlotte.

KEVIN: Yes . . . Great.

Silence.

I've got the van outside. Waiting!

CHARLOTTE: Yes. (*She sips her orange juice.*)

KEVIN: Yes. She's completely ready. Tuned up. I've tuned her up. She'll give us a fantastic ride. Yes – we'll be really safe inside her.

CHARLOTTE: Good. (*Very delicately.*) Do you think I could have another straw, this one's got a little dirty . . .

KEVIN: A dirty straw! They're probably all really dirty straws in a place like this, probably been used several times before. (*He reaches for a glass of straws, knocks it over.*)

KEVIN (*smiles*): That tends to happen.

CHARLOTTE *picks it up quickly and takes a straw.*

Have you got a straw?

CHARLOTTE (*shyly*): Yes. Thank you very much. (*She starts to drink again out of the new straw.*)

KEVIN (*staring at her drinking*): Got a straw now, have you?

CHARLOTTE (*surprised*): Yes!

KEVIN: Great.

Pause.

I'm very early aren't I?

CHARLOTTE: No, you're exactly on time, I think.

KEVIN (*grins*): Am I? Looking forward to it are you?

CHARLOTTE: Yes, in a way.

KEVIN: Yeah. So am I. Where are we going first?

CHARLOTTE: Hertfordshire.

KEVIN: Great. I've got the 'literature' and everything. It's all ready – it looks really good, really clear, I'm quite proud of it. Yes! They're all expecting us, are they?

CHARLOTTE: Yes, of course.

KEVIN: Great.

Pause.

Got the list and everything, have you?

CHARLOTTE: Yes. (*She taps her bag.*) In here.

KEVIN: Great. (*He smiles at her.*) Guard it carefully, won't you?

CHARLOTTE: Of course. (*Shy smile.*) Naturally.

KEVIN: I've got hundreds of maps – yes, the whole country! Every inch, M1, M6, M18 *all the roads.* Want a cup cake? (*He fishes into his pockets.*) I've got some somewhere. One chocolate, two banana flavour . . . (*Smiles.*) Where are they? May have melted, of course in this weather. (*Grins.*) Maybe I'll find they've run down my trouser leg. Sorry.

CHARLOTTE: No, thank you anyway.

KEVIN (*looking at her*): Nervous, are you?

CHARLOTTE: Slightly, I think. I don't know . . . a little.

KEVIN: Your first time is it?

CHARLOTTE: Yes.

KEVIN: Mine too. No need to be nervous, no need at all. (*He smiles.*) Perhaps we ought to go for a swim instead, much better. One of those days your arse, your bottom sticks to the leather of the seat, isn't it! You'll like the smell of leather in the van, you know, that smell of really old leather, it's a great smell, gets you like a drug, old wooden dashboard too, fantastic, really ace one, with an extraordinarily roomy glove compartment, enormous! Like a tunnel. You can reach for miles, up to your armpit.

Pause. He smiles.

Sorry.

CHARLOTTE: We ought to leave in four minutes. (*She takes out a yoghurt, begins to eat.*)

KEVIN: Soon as that? (*He watches her.*) What you got there in your hand?

CHARLOTTE (*looks surprised*): It's my yoghurt. (*She stares at him.*) You ought to wear real spectacles, I think.

KEVIN (*broad smile*): Yeah – I only wish I could.

Silence. CHARLOTTE watches him.

CHARLOTTE: We've met before once, haven't we?

KEVIN: Yes – at the winter meeting, I think. I sat on the radiator. And you may have seen me duplicating.

CHARLOTTE (*starting right at him*): You're the one that has trouble with his eyes.

KEVIN: That's right. I've trouble with my eyes. Yes – a little.

CHARLOTTE: But you can see all right, can't you . . . I mean.

KEVIN: Oh yes, yes, I can see all right.

Pause.

But I'm going blind . . . maybe.

CHARLOTTE: Blind? (CHARLOTTE

is calm; she stares at him.) I'm sorry to hear that.

KEVIN (*genuine smile*): So was I. It's a disease you know – of the retina. So all could be blackness up here – (*He taps his eyes.*) – quite soon.

CHARLOTTE: I'm sorry.

KEVIN (*smiles*): No, no need to be. We ought to have a coffee now – sharpen us up for it.

CHARLOTTE: No, thank you very much, but I don't drink coffee.

KEVIN: The thing is . . . what's worrying me, about our journey . . . is, my driving licence is a bit out of date. Two years out of date.

CHARLOTTE: Why? (*Astonished.*) Why didn't you have it renewed?

Pause.

KEVIN: I forgot.

CHARLOTTE: And anyway, one's not really meant to drive at all if one can't see. (*She looks at KEVIN.*) Is one?

KEVIN: You're right about that . . .

CHARLOTTE: Then what happens if we're stopped . . .

KEVIN: Stopped by whom?

CHARLOTTE: The police, of course.

KEVIN: They won't stop us. (*He smiles.*) They won't know I can't see, will they? I'm a very safe driver, I am in fact – I just keep going in a straight line.

CHARLOTTE: I'll drive, I think.

KEVIN: You can drive?

CHARLOTTE: Yes – a little.

KEVIN: A little.

CHARLOTTE: Enough . . .

KEVIN: OK then. Why not? (*He pulls out the keys, holds them.*) But the whole *point* of me *being here* was to drive the van.

CHARLOTTE: I know. (*She smiles.*) But we don't want to get killed, do we?

KEVIN: No. You're right, of course. Here. (*He hands her the keys.*)

CHARLOTTE: I hope you don't mind me asking, but it's important . . . I mean, what can you see?

KEVIN: Well, I can see you . . .

CHARLOTTE: Good, that's a start.

KEVIN: You've got black hair, haven't you? (CHARLOTTE *is blonde*.) Short cropped black hair.

(*Pause. KEVIN gives a broad smile.*)

Actually you haven't. Don't worry. I know you haven't. Only a joke, it's apricot, a sort of apricot.

CHARLOTTE (*staring hard*): Yes. I've just had it cut, actually.

Pause.

KEVIN (*suddenly looks nervously over his shoulder then back at her*): Sorry – just having a look, that feeling gets to you, doesn't it, a sort of buzz down here. (*He feels the pit of his stomach.*) Christ! (*He suddenly smiles.*) Any moment we'll be speeding along, actually starting on it. I've got a camera with me. *And* some film. Be able to record it all. It's great weather for it anyway.

CHARLOTTE: You're very warmly dressed for it, aren't you?

KEVIN: Am I? (*He smiles.*) I don't like taking clothes off in public. I even sunbathe in a mackintosh.

CHARLOTTE: Do you really?

He glances at her.

KEVIN: You're not wearing sandals anyway.

CHARLOTTE: How do you know I'm not wearing sandals?

KEVIN: I can feel under the table.

CHARLOTTE: Yes. (*She smiles.*) I don't usually wear sandals.

KEVIN (*suddenly*): I saw a film once, it was only half an hour, but it was all of feet, feet crawling, feet eating, feet running over marshy ground and things, even over hot coals, getting burnt, that wasn't so nice. Just gone through my mind, you see. (*He smiles.*) Sorry, those pre-journey nerves again. (*Suddenly, a shrewd look.*) You're a little keyed-up, aren't you, but not showing it. Don't worry about it. (*He moves.*) (*Fast:*) Yeah. I used to go to the movies a lot you see, more than just a lot really. I went every day for two years. Almost. You know, see all the movies – (*He indicates his eyes.*) – before these run out . . .

CHARLOTTE *gives a slight, amused smile.*

Go ahead. I don't mind people laughing . . .

CHARLOTTE: I wasn't. I wouldn't laugh at something like that.

KEVIN: No, honestly, I don't mind people laughing, it's no skin off my elbow. (*Friendly smile.*) It really isn't. (*He looks at the table.*) Filthy here, isn't it, in this cafe, start of the road! A bit of fried egg here on the table – full of stains.

CHARLOTTE: Yes it is.

KEVIN: Imagine when the holocaust comes and these places are all deserted and there are thistles growing on the motorway . . . and there's grass growing over the jukebox . . . and honeysuckle coming out of the expresso, yeah . . . and tadpoles swimming in the ladies.

CHARLOTTE (*amused smile*): Yes – I can imagine.

KEVIN: And of course there'll be a new sort of beast that hatches its eggs in the remains of the stale chips, yeah, in the chip trays, it lays its small blue eggs everywhere, all over, this new beast, and suddenly . . . and then suddenly it emerges from the fryers, this monster covered in batter, whole body in batter, and it goes after the last humans, catching and eating them. (*He smiles.*) We'd be among the survivors of course.

CHARLOTTE: Yes, of course.

KEVIN: Great scenario isn't it, for a B movie. Scenario de Bergerac.

CHARLOTTE: Yes. It's time now.

KEVIN: Sorry. I'm sorry – I'm talking shit, don't usually talk as much as this, must be annoying you.

CHARLOTTE: No. It's not.

KEVIN: It's just nerves you know. (*Self-mocking smile.*) Not that I'm nervous, of course.

CHARLOTTE: No.

KEVIN (*brushing himself*): It's just so dusty in here.

CHARLOTTE: I have a few of these if you like, moistened tissues.

CHARLOTTE *passes a tissue to* KEVIN.

KEVIN: Thanks, yeah. (*He wipes his face.*) Great things these.
Now I feel ready for anything.
We ought to get you some dark glasses too, oughtn't we, for the journey?

CHARLOTTE (*smiles*): Then we'd certainly get stopped, wouldn't we . . .

KEVIN: Yes, maybe. We mustn't get stopped . . . (*He grins.*) Not a good idea.

CHARLOTTE: Shall we . . .

KEVIN (*jumps up*): Yes! (*He moves over to the jukebox.*) I think we'd just better have a record for the road, don't you? Get us in the mood. (*He crosses over.*) Get us travelling well – speeding along . . . we're going the whole way . . . (*He selects a nostalgic Beach Boys standard.*)

(KEVIN *picks up his bag.*) Nice! It brings back memories, doesn't it? Let's leave. (*He doesn't move.*) Gets one, doesn't it . . . No, come on – let's leave!

CHARLOTTE *leaves a tip on the table and picks up her bag.*

(KEVIN *is staring about him with feeling.*) This cafe could be anywhere, couldn't it? This view – this smell, the traffic out there – not just London – we could be anywhere on earth.

CHARLOTTE (*glancing round*): No it couldn't.

KEVIN (*quiet*): No. (*Then he grins.*) Ready? Prepared?

CHARLOTTE: Yes.

KEVIN: Great!

Blackout

Scene Two

The verge. NICK *blond hair, in his early twenties, stands staring down at them. Sound of traffic very loud, then quieter dying in and out of scene.* KEVIN *and* CHARLOTTE *are sitting with their picnic basket, and a small vat of ice-cream, a bottle of mineral water, a camera, an umbrella, and a book lying beside the picnic basket.*

KEVIN (*staring at the ice-cream*): We better have it now, don't you think or it'll melt.

CHARLOTTE (*glances round at him*): You're always wanting to eat, aren't you?

KEVIN (*smiling*): No. No I'm not. But I bought this specially. See, mocha almond fudge, lots of it. (*He lifts the lid slightly.*)

NICK (*calls down at them*): Hey!

KEVIN: We don't have to have it now, if you don't want. Save it till later. Easy. (*He moves the vat of ice-cream.*) It's nice and cold anyway.

CHARLOTTE (*quietly to herself*): I've got to phone home at some point. I mustn't forget. I've got to phone mother. (*She glances at him.*) Why don't you eat it if you want some – go on!

KEVIN (*lifts the lid of the ice-cream*): I don't know . . .

NICK (*very loud*): Hey!

They turn and see him.

KEVIN: Yes?

NICK *moves closer.*

NICK: I . . . (*He smiles.*) I saw you get out of that van just now, the old one back there.

KEVIN: Yes, that's the one – she's just being filled up.

NICK: And I just wondered – (*He smiles, looks from one to the other.*) – which way you're going?

KEVIN: Which way we're going? (*He glances at* CHARLOTTE.)

NICK: Are you going north by any chance . . . ?

KEVIN: You mean up the motorway?

NICK: Yes – are you?

KEVIN: Yes, I think we are. We're going that way. (*He indicates.*)

NICK: That's north.

CHARLOTTE (*sharp*): Yes we know.

KEVIN *opens the lid of the ice-cream.*

KEVIN: I think we'll have the ice-cream now don't you, get it open, before it disappears.

NICK: And I was wondering – (*He smiles.*) – just wondering if you had any room?

KEVIN (*looking up*): Any room?

NICK (*irritated*): Yes.

KEVIN: You mean in the van?

NICK: Yes, for a lift.

KEVIN: No, we don't have any room at all. I'm sorry, we're full up.

NICK (*quieter, smiles*): With what?

CHARLOTTE (*suddenly sharp*): We're full. (*She's drinking out of a bottle, but with a straw, delicately.*)

NICK: Sorry, OK, thanks. (*He moves slightly, then stops.*)

CHARLOTTE: Is there anything else you want . . . ?

NICK: No.

KEVIN (*looking towards CHARLOTTE*)' We don't mean to be rude, we're just full up. Want an egg? Got hundreds of boiled eggs here?

NICK: OK. (*He Smiles.*) Thanks very much.

KEVIN: I'll peel it for you. (*He begins to peel it very slowly.*) This heat's so heavy isn't it, hottest summer there's ever been. (*He glances behind him.*) Can hardly see the pylon back there – through the haze.

CHARLOTTE: Hardly, no.

KEVIN: The road may melt, of course, in a moment. No, seriously, roads are melting now, traffic, slushing around in hot black tar. Just look at it, you can smell it from here, it's already starting to bubble a little. (*Pause.*) Not a pretty sight. Great setting for a modern-day Western wouldn't it?

NICK (*smiles, amused*): Yes I suppose it would be. (*He glances with an amused grin.*) People galloping along the freeway, keeping to their different lanes, lassooing everything. (*He smiles.*) Yes . . .

KEVIN (*smiles at him*): Yeah . . . sorry we couldn't help you.

NICK: That's OK.

KEVIN *puts the egg he was peeling for NICK into his own mouth.*

CHARLOTTE: Careful Kevin – it's still got the shell on.

KEVIN: OK thanks – I thought I'd got it all off. (*He looks at NICK.*) I was doing it for you, wasn't I, anyway. Here do one for yourself. (*He stretches to give NICK an egg and knocks over the mineral-water bottle; NICK catches it.*)

NICK: There!

KEVIN: Thanks.

NICK: Lucky it had the top on, isn't it.

KEVIN: I'll try the ice-cream shall I – hope for more success. (*He scoops at the ice-cream.*)

NICK (*watching them*): Where you going?

CHARLOTTE: Scotland.

NICK: That's nice isn't it. (*He smiles, watching them.*) I'm going to Scotland too actually, as it happens.

KEVIN (*hardly listening*): And back. We going there and back.

NICK: Visiting relatives you see.

KEVIN (*ignoring him*): Great. That's great. Here try that. Mocha almond fudge. (*He holds out a cone with ice-cream.*) Should be OK.

NICK: Thanks. (*He takes the cone and licks it.*)

KEVIN: How is it?

NICK: Yes, fine. (*He takes another cautious lick.*) Tastes a little of petrol but it's fine.

KEVIN: Petrol?

NICK: Yes – just a little.

KEVIN: Can't taste of petrol can it?

NICK *squats, picks up the book.*

CHARLOTTE: Careful of the ants – they're everywhere.

NICK: Yes, of course I will.

He flicks the pages of the book;
CHARLOTTE *is tense.*

KEVIN: Must be my hands if it tastes of it. Nasty stuff petrol . . . occupational hazard you know.

NICK (*amused*): I quite understand. (*He licks the ice-cream.*) It's very nice really.

CHARLOTTE (*she picks up a piece of litter*): Careful of mess.

KEVIN: Yeah. (*Suddenly pushing his hand into the ground:*) I wonder what's underneath here, under the ground, probably a drainage system, a whole network of shafts, five hundred, a thousand feet deep, going right into the heart of it. Maybe something in them as well. All the rubbish. Tons of it. Bound to be. Dead animals and things, maybe a dead body even. One never knows what's underneath the earth, does one?

NICK (*puzzled*): No . . .

KEVIN: Could be anything.

The roar of a jet overhead – really loud and screeching; they all look up and shade their eyes.

KEVIN: See it! Can you see it!

NICK: Yes! It's very low.

CHARLOTTE: It's a really large one.

KEVIN (*suddenly shouts*): Get away! Go on!
You want to stretch out your hand, don't you – pull it down, put it out of the sky. We *would be* eating under a flight path.

The noise begins to die.

KEVIN: I once went to a concert near here. I used to travel round England a lot you see. Great concert round here somewhere, you know outdoors, years ago.

NICK (*smiles lightly*): Yes, I can remember all that too.

KEVIN: I don't remember the planes though. Sorry – nostalgia corner there! Take a picture shall I – (*He jumps up, picks up the camera.*) – of this haze. Better use the camera since it's here. (*He lifts the camera.*) A landscape. (*He clicks, moves his position.*) There! Easy! A landscape with road! (*He clicks again.*) Great shots.

NICK: Yes!

KEVIN: It's good to keep a record. See what's happening in the countryside. Yeah, be great to put a camera in the truck, keep filming as we move, whole lot of images moving along the road, filming everything.

NICK: Don't forget to wind on the film.

CHARLOTTE: That's right, did you wind it on Kevin?

KEVIN: I have now. (*He does so.*) Take one of you Charlotte, shall I?

CHARLOTTE: No, thank you.

KEVIN: Come on, don't be shy.

CHARLOTTE: I am shy – I'm not at all photogenic. People are always teasing me.

KEVIN: No, come on, it'll be great. Just one picture. Come on, no keep still.

CHARLOTTE: Please Kevin – I'm asking you, I *don't want* my picture taken. And you're embarrassing me in front of strangers.

NICK: I'll turn my back – (*He smiles.*) I'm not watching. (*But he doesn't move.*)

KEVIN: One, two, three, nothing to be afraid of.

He snaps; CHARLOTTE *jolts.*

You moved!

NICK (*watching, amused smile*): Why you going to Scotland?

KEVIN (*winding on the film*): What?

NICK: Why you going?

KEVIN: Business.

CHARLOTTE: And a very short holiday.

NICK: What . . . if you don't mind me asking . . . what sort of business?

KEVIN: What sort? Just business, that sort.

NICK: I see. (*He smiles, glances at the book he's holding.*)

CHARLOTTE: Are you reading that book, because if not . . .

NICK (*smiling*): No – does it look like it?

Awkward atmosphere. They watch him.

I mean, sorry to be curious, what's the van full of?

KEVIN: Packages.

NICK: Packages of what?

They look at him.

Sorry, I'm just interested.

CHARLOTTE: Packages of leaflets.

NICK (*flicks one out of the book, from a wadge which is between its pages*): Is this one of them?

KEVIN: What's that?

NICK: They're lots in this book.

KEVIN: Yeah – that's one of them. (*He looks at* CHARLOTTE.) There's no reason why he shouldn't know is there? Don't muck it up will you?

NICK: Can I read it?

CHARLOTTE: If you have to . . . if you're really interested.

NICK glances at the leaflet.

KEVIN: They're nicely printed this time aren't they?

CHARLOTTE: Yes.

NICK (*surprised*): The English People's Party!!

KEVIN: Yes – that's what we are.

NICK (*grins*): What? All two of you.

Silence.

I'm afraid I haven't heard of it. Is it new?

CHARLOTTE: Not all that new, no.

NICK (*begins to read the leaflet, they watch him intently*): I see . . . (*He suddenly laughs.*) Fucking hell! (*He reads, skipping through the leaflet.*) Have you thought about England lately, England now . . . the ordinary, long-suffering English people. *Pollution . . . the length and breadth of England polluted, every river, every field!* Pollution on a gigantic scale. *Urban Wastelands –* (*He smiles.*) *–* the sad urban wastelands, disaster of our city centres . . . too many people crammed together like mice. (*He grins.*) LIKE MICE! . . . leading to distressing violence, criminal town and population planning. *Impersonal Government –* ordinary people offered no chance or choice, crushed by impersonal government. *The Mauling of the Countryside –* the countryside has been mauled . . . disastrous series of mistakes . . . the worship of the motor car . . . internal combustion engine eaten away the fabric of the country, the very fabric of ordinary people's lives destroyed. Preserve . . . exclamation mark . . . Preserve. (*He turns the page.*) Preserve.

Silence. He smiles.

This is pretty heavy isn't it? Are you really distributing this?

CHARLOTTE: Yes.

NICK (*amused*): You two . . . Both of you together.

KEVIN: That's right.

NICK: Going up the road, handing these out.

CHARLOTTE: Yes. What's the matter?

NICK (*smiling*): It's just a little surprising finding you two picnicking by the motorway . . . and doing this. (*He looks at the leaflet with a broad smile.* So it's conservation, and kill the motor car.

CHARLOTTE (*looking at* KEVIN): He's not really interested.

NICK: Of course I am. Can I keep this?

CHARLOTTE: Only if you're really interested.

KEVIN: I think we better clear up, hadn't we?

HARLOTTE: Yes, we're five minutes behind schedule.

ICK: Schedule! (*He grins.*) You've got a schedule?

HARLOTTE: Yes, thank you. do you think you could pick that up? (*She points to the ice-cream cone he's left lying; NICK picks it up.*) It's just litter's not very nice, is it?

EVIN: Even by a motorway. Right. I'll take the picnic basket, shall I? (*He picks it up.*) Nice meeting you, mate. Have a good trip. Good luck. (*He goes.*)

ICK (*picks up another piece of litter, puts it in her plastic litter bag*): There.

HARLOTTE: That's right. Could you pass me the mineral water, please.

ICK: There.

CHARLOTTE *sits, methodically rolls back her sleeve.*

HARLOTTE: The sun doesn't do me any good.

ICK (*watching, smiles*): It looks as if you're going to give yourself an injection.

HARLOTTE: Don't be stupid. Please don't talk like that. (*She lifts the mineral water, suddenly splashes it over her arm.*) That's better.

ICK: Are you – (*He laughs.*) Are you really on this English People's Party trip?

HARLOTTE: We told you, yes.

ICK(*smiles*): I don't quite believe you.

CHARLOTTE *picks up the litter.*

HARLOTTE (*detached*): And what do you do?

ICK: I'm trying to be a teacher.

HARLOTTE: Good. (*Not unpleasant:*) I hope you find work.

ICK: And you're going all the way up the country.

HARLOTTE: Yes.

ICK: I'm going that way myself.

IARLOTTE: So we gathered.

NICK (*picks up another piece of litter, big smile*): There.

CHARLOTTE: Thank you. Do you always try to force yourself on people for free lifts?

NICK: Yes. Quite often. Yes.

CHARLOTTE (*not unpleasant*): Must make you popular, mustn't it. (*Holding her bag:*) Do you want the eggs? No. You can have them. We'll give them to you.

NICK (*laughing, amused*): No, thank you.

KEVIN *enters.*

KEVIN: There! Ready? Prepared?

CHARLOTTE: Yes.

KEVIN: I must find my shoes. (*He glances round.*)

NICK: Here they are! They're here. (*He finds them for* KEVIN.)

KEVIN: Great. Thanks. Knock the insects out. (*He does so.*)

NICK: How about as far as Nottingham?

Slight pause.

CHARLOTTE: I don't think so.

They move to go.

NICK: Won't you be needing these.

They turn.

Your car keys. (*He holds them up.*)

KEVIN: Oh great – thanks. We ought to have those. Yeah.

NICK: You would have left them behind wouldn't you? (*He holds them.*) Do I get a lift now, just as far as Nottingham.

Pause.

Come on, why not? It won't cost you anything.

KEVIN: No . . . but . . .

NICK: Why not. I won't be in the way of anything, will I.

KEVIN (*casual*): No . . . but . . .

NICK: And you could always try to convert me, couldn't you?

KEVIN: Are you really interested?

NICK: In a way.

Pause.

KEVIN: OK. Why not. To Nottingham then.

NICK (*smiles*): Here.

NICK *tosses the keys*, KEVIN *completely misses them.* CHARLOTTE *stops, looking for them.*

There . . . to your left.

KEVIN *goes to his right.*

No, to your left.

KEVIN: Yes. (*He picks them up. They stare at* NICK.) Great.

Blackout

Scene Three

The sun lounge. Muzak rising and falling. CHARLOTTE *and* KEVIN. MRS ROBERTS *sitting, nervously flicking through a magazine; she's in her late thirties, good-looking. She's surrounded by shopping bags.*

CHARLOTTE (*staring behind her*): Has he come up? (*She turns to* KEVIN.) Has he?

KEVIN: Yes, he's just behind you.

CHARLOTTE *swings round as* NICK *enters.*

CHARLOTTE: We said Bedford, didn't we. You'd leave at Bedford.

NICK (*grins*): I know.

CHARLOTTE (*moving down to* KEVIN): I wish he'd go away.

KEVIN: It'll be all right – he'll leave.

CHARLOTTE (*staring down at* MRS ROBERTS): There she is, anyway.

KEVIN: Where?

CHARLOTTE: Over there.

KEVIN: You sure that's her?

CHARLOTTE: Yes.

KEVIN: The one on the list?

CHARLOTTE: Yes. (*She turns towards* NICK.) If you have to be here, please be polite.

NICK: Of course.

They approach MRS ROBERTS.

CHARLOTTE: Hello, Mrs Roberts.

MRS ROBERTS *flicks round and stares up at her.*

It is Mrs Roberts?

MRS ROBERTS: Yes, yes it is.

CHARLOTTE: I'm terribly sorry we're so late.

KEVIN: We had a bit of a picnic you see.

NICK (*staring behind him*): God, it's enormous back there, isn't it?

MRS ROBERTS: That's perfectly all right of course. How do you do . . .?

CHARLOTTE (*they shake hands*): I'm Charlotte. We met very briefly before. The February meeting.

MRS ROBERTS: That's right – yes.

CHARLOTTE: This is Kevin Gellot.

KEVIN: Hello. Great to meet you.

MRS ROBERTS: Yes. (*She glances towards* NICK *who is standing some distance away.*)

CHARLOTTE: He's nobody. He managed to cadge a free lift off us; we'll be dropping him off.

MRS ROBERTS: Yes, I thought meeting on the road was best, so you didn't have to leave the motorway. And it's always empty, here in the sun lounge.

NICK (*smiles*): The sun lounge . . .

The muzak cuts out. An announcement comes over the speakers: 'The coach to Newcastle will be leaving in three minutes, please take your seats'.

MRS ROBERTS (*looks round at the speakers*): I have to listen out . . . For my coach. Do you want anything? Some tea? Some chocolate. I could go and fetch some.

CHARLOTTE: That's awfully kind – no thank you.

MRS ROBERTS: Do sit down . . . please.

CHARLOTTE: Thank you.

MRS ROBERTS *looks anxiously at NICK.*

NICK: I'll stand, thank you. I'm only here to watch.

KEVIN (*staring out*): It's incredible here – the glass is thick. Can hardly hear the traffic, just watch it.

MRS ROBERTS: I know, there was an accident last time I was here and nobody heard it. It was extraordinary really.

NICK (*smiles*): It's just like an airport in here isn't it.?

KEVIN (*serious, staring out*): Yeah . . .

MRS ROBERTS (*glancing up*): It's all right for you here is it: (*She smiles.*) I do hope it's all right. We can manage here I think, do what we have to do. I mean it's quite nice here, have you seen the pictures on the walls, the pictures of England everywhere, some beautiful views, and on *all* the ashtrays and the mats. See, (*She indicates the mats.*) and brochures too. (*She shows CHARLOTTE.*) Even in the passage-ways and the toilets. (*She smiles.*) Quite fun really, isn't it? And there's lots of sun for you today.

CHARLOTTE: Of course. It's perfect. (*She laughs a short laugh. She picks up a mat.*) They're lovely, that's one of home I think, the North Downs.

KEVIN (*staring down*): See, look at that one, so bulging with oil, hardly can get round the bend.

NICK: You don't like traffic, do you?

Over the speakers: 'The coach to Newcastle will depart in one minute. Take your seats'.

MRS ROBERTS (*suddenly urgent*): I mustn't miss the coach back. That would be terrible – I have to fetch the children.

CHARLOTTE: Yes, how are they?

MRS ROBERTS: They're well thank you. A lot of bother of course. The eldest, Barbara, she's always going off, she's a lot of bother, I hardly ever see her. The baby's very well. The other two – (*She smiles.*) – they're becoming a little difficult too of course . . . oh yes. They're very well. (*She looks at the speakers.*) But I know you want to get down to business. I know you're very short of time . . . and so am I. We must do it. (*She looks at NICK.*)

NICK (*smiles*): Yes . . . I'll – (*He grins.*) I'll make myself scarce, shall I? I'll play the machines. That's OK is it? I have a habit of winning on these. (*He moves over to two fruit machines standing side by side.*)

CHARLOTTE: Don't worry about him.

MRS ROBERTS: Yes, this is a quiet corner anyway – it's so big here. There's always a corner where you can be unnoticed. And there're hardly any black waiters, or black waitresses, which is extraordinary isn't it. (*She smiles nicely.*) But they don't seem to have them here. (*She suddenly turns in her seat.*) Sorry, I'm a little worried about missing my coach.

A loud buzz is heard through the muzak, then a voice: 'The coach to Newcastle has left, the coach to Newcastle has now left'.

MRS ROBERTS (*glancing at CHARLOTTE*): There's not much time to go you know.

KEVIN (*suddenly, still staring out*): I went to a concert near here.

MRS ROBERTS (*to herself*): Oh yes.

KEVIN: An open air concert, a long time ago now. It was a festival. A huge one. And at the end, the last evening we walked back along here, down the motorway, right down here, brought the whole road to a standstill. There were jugglers, people lighting bonfires along the way, sword swallowers, a whole fayre. It was three miles long, a great sight, a huge column, and a whole colourful army of it.

NICK: Three lemons and a cherry. Four-teen! Fourteen! You see I always win.

KEVIN: Can almost see it now. And hear it. Then fade back, fade back to the road, the roar of the traffic, back to . . . now. We're going all the way up that road.

The loudspeakers: 'The coach to Crewe will leave in three minutes. The coach to Crewe will leave in three minutes. Please take your seats'.

MRS ROBERTS (*looking towards* KEVIN): We ought to get on.

CHARLOTTE: Why don't you join him, Kevin, just for a moment. Play the machine.

NICK (*calling*): Yes, come and try to win!

KEVIN: Great! Of course.

CHARLOTTE (*to* MRS ROBERTS, *as* KEVIN *goes to the machines*): There's our latest circular for you to read. The membership's rising you know, through word of mouth, and our advertisements have been successful. They've done very well.

MRS ROBERTS (*takes the circular*): Thank you.

KEVIN: I used to know somebody that could get these machines to pay up, just by tickling them. Like tickling fish. Yeah, they loved it, it was great, they coughed up like anything, they loved it. (*He rubs the handle of the machine in masturbatory fashion.*)

NICK (*laughs*): Hey! What you doing?

KEVIN (*grins*): Sorry about that, bit of crudity for you there.

MRS ROBERTS (*having glanced at the circular*): Thank you. That's good news. I came here last week as well you know, on party business.

CHARLOTTE: Did you?

MRS ROBERTS: It's good to get out of town for once. It was my husband's night out. I took the coach, full of people shouting and screaming, as you can imagine.

CHARLOTTE: Yes.

MRS ROBERTS: I got Eileen from next door, she's a very excitable girl, but she came round to mind the kids.

NICK: Four strawberries. Sixteen! Sixteen! Don't do that Kevin.

KEVIN (*wrenching at the handle*): I never win.

MRS ROBERTS: I came here to meet a schoolmaster, a Mr Godfrey. He's a very nice man, very well-mannered. You wouldn't know him but . . .

The speaker: 'The coach to Crewe will depart in one minute. The coach to Crewe will depart in one minute. Take your seats'.

MRS ROBERTS (*swings rounds as the announcement is made*): Sorry, I just mustn't miss my coach. We have so little time, but I must tell you this, may I, quickly (*Fast:*) . . . Mr Godfrey, you see, I came here to meet him. He's a teacher at the comprehensive. He teaches Latin and French, I think it is, he's a very clever man, he feels things strongly. There's a few of them at that school who do. It's nice isn't it, to meet somebody that feels things strongly, instead of just muddle.

CHARLOTTE: Of course.

NICK: Four cherries. There we go – another eight!

KEVIN: Don't know how you do it.

MRS ROBERTS: I came here to meet him. *But he didn't turn up.* I don't know why – maybe he couldn't get away. I was here, in this very seat, for hours and hours waiting. It was night, you get some rather strange people about at that time you know, their faces coming up to you.

KEVIN (*by the machine*): I never win anything.

MRS ROBERTS (*fast*): I went and asked them to call him over the speakers. Call Mr Godfrey, see if he was somewhere in this huge place, in a corner somewhere. But they wouldn't. (*Urgent:*) I tried to phone him too – tell you this too, if there's time . . . it's good to talk to you, you know – I tried to phone him. There're eighteen telephones back there, I don't know if you can see them, I went to call him, and fourteen of them, no, fifteen of the phones were out of order. You lifted them up and they made this really terrible whining noise, nearly blows your head off you know – (*She smiles.*) – like a scream almost. You know what I mean. Fifteen of them. I left all the receivers off, one by one, let them make the noise, to draw attention to it. I think it was worth doing.

CHARLOTTE: Yes, of course.

MRS ROBERTS: There's so little time, I know . . . (*She glances over her shoulder.*) – but can I tell you this too, I think I can. (*She looks at the loud-speakers.*) You see I had rather a strange experience when I was here then . . .

NICK *and* KEVIN *return.*

NICK (*grins*): I won over a pound.

KEVIN: He's really lucky – really really lucky. They just poured out for him.

NICK (*smiles*): I'm always lucky.

CHARLOTTE (*to* NICK): Ssssh . . . Mrs Roberts.

MRS ROBERTS: Don't you want to sit down . . . I was telling Charlotte . . .

The speakers: 'The coach to Crewe has left. The coach to Crewe has now left'.

(*Louder:*) Yes! I had to wait such a long time here last week and I had . . . I'll show you – (*She gets up.*) – if you excuse me . . .

NICK *moves out of the way.*

You don't mind me showing you. (*She moves over to the radiator.*) I was alone here you see, by myself, by this radiator, and then I saw a little smoke coming out of it. I smelled this strange heat, and saw this piece of smoke. (*She smiles.*) It was coming out, you see. (*She shows with her hand.*) And I saw here – (*She feels in the radiator.*) – there was this long plastic thing lying in the radiator smoking. (*Lightly:*) I thought it was a bomb put there. Of course I shouted. They came – after a long time.
They said it wasn't a bomb, I didn't

know whether to believe them, whether they were just saying that. It was frightening of course. They scraped it away, scraped it off. (*She feels with her hand, then pulls it back.*) I think there's some there now, a little left. Yes. (*She smiles.*) Whatever it is. (*She smiles at them.*) I've told you now.

CHARLOTTE: Yes, it must have been unpleasant.

KEVIN: Oh yes.

MRS ROBERTS: I think, I really think people who do that, leave bombs and think up these terrible hoaxes, have to be really dealt with now. I think they have to be shot really. (*She smiles.*) Don't they? Shot on sight.

The speakers: 'The coach to London will leave in two minutes. The coach to London will leave in two minutes. Please take your seats'.

MRS ROBERTS: It's not my coach, but the next one will be. I have to get that one, can't let the kids get the school bus – they're all so violent on a Friday, all the kids, aren't they?
Come on quickly, where's my bag? (*She scrambles with her bags.*) We must do it now, mustn't we, quickly I know. It's all in here. (*She opens a large bag.*) This is just . . . just a book of cuttings, I thought you'd like to see. (*It is a book like a child's album.*)

NICK (*smiles*): A book of cuttings?

CHARLOTTE (*to* NICK): Don't you want to play those machines again?

NICK: No, not now.

MRS ROBERTS: I stick things in here, to keep a record, so I remember what's happening in the world. It's not very complete I'm afraid.

KEVIN: Great! Look she's stuck every-thing in there.

MRS ROBERTS (*opening the scrap-book*): There's Mr Relph of course, the Relph case, you know, the case of his board, his notice, you know about that of course. Then there's the piece about trouble at the comprehensive. A stabbing – a black boy did there. It's extraordinary what goes on, isn't it? I mean you notice it all the time, I'm not that particular, but you can't walk down the street without them running into you, hitting you and things, on Saturdays especially. (*She smiles.*) Mostly black boys of course – but not all by any means I'm afraid. I got bruised three times last week. (*She begins to roll her sleeve back.*) Bruised rather badly. I'm sorry to go on, but I better show you, if there's time, I'm not sure there is, but . . .

The speakers: 'The coach to London has now left'. She finishes rolling her sleeve up.

You can see them down my arm, right down my arm I'm afraid.

CHARLOTTE: Yes, that's horrible.

MRS ROBERTS (*smiles*): And I'm afraid it does hurt. It does really hurt rather a lot. (*Louder:*) It still does!

KEVIN (*looking at her arm*): Yes, that must do.

NICK (*staring at her*): Are you a member of the National Front.

MRS ROBERTS (*looks up*): Yes, yes I am.

NICK: Christ. (*He stares at CHARLOTTE.*) Did you hear that?

MRS ROBERTS (*rolling down her sleeve*): Sorry I know I shouldn't have bothered you with that. I just wanted to tell you, you see. My coach is coming now, any moment they'll call it. So here! Before it comes, here it all is. (*She rummages in her bag.*) The things I've got . . . I don't know if they'll come in useful. This is – (*She pulls out a crumpled parcel.*) . . . this is an eletroset, that's what the name is isn't it. It was going so cheap, I thought you might want it.

CHARLOTTE: Thank you, that's marvellous, isn't that good Kevin?

KEVIN: Yes, that's great.

MRS ROBERTS: And this is – (*She pulls it out of her bag.*) . . . here's some wire, a large roll, see, strong wire. I don't know if it'll come in

useful. But it's very strong.

NICK (*astonished*): Wire! What's that for

CHARLOTTE: Thank you very much. That's wonderful.

MRS ROBERTS: And here we are now, here it is. There. (*She pulls out of the bag a wadge of bank notes wrapped in the sort of paper cheese is wrapped in.*) There's £83 and 40 pence. I'm very sorry, I thought it was going to be more. I thought we were going to manage at least £110, but it's only £83. Do you want to count it, you better do it quickly, I expect you do, don't you?

CHARLOTTE: No, that's all right thank you.

MRS ROBERTS: Not nearly as much as we hoped. It's so difficult to get people to keep their word isn't it? I hope you're not too disappointed. I know I was terribly.

CHARLOTTE: No, of course we're not. (*With the money.*) That's wonderful, isn't it Kevin?

KEVIN: Yes that's great. It's a lot.

MRS ROBERTS: I don't feel that it's nearly enough really.

NICK (*suddenly*): Why are you a member of two organisations Mrs Roberts?

MRS ROBERTS: What? (*She looks up at him.*) What did you say?

The speakers: 'The coach to Preston will depart in one minute. The coach to Preston will depart in one minute. Take your seats'.

MRS ROBERTS: That's it now! That's my coach. Why have they only given us one minute now.

CHARLOTTE: Here's the receipt for the money.

MRS ROBERTS: Of course thank you – if I miss the coach – I don't know what will happen about the kids.

CHARLOTTE: Kevin, maybe you could help Mrs Roberts?

KEVIN: Of course. Here, I'll take those, no trouble at all.

MRS ROBERTS: Thank you. It's always such a rush now isn't it? Everything just one long rush. So nice seeing you, being able to talk, even for so short a time. I'm sorry I didn't have more for you.

KEVIN *moves off.*

Bye Bye. (*As she leaves:*) It is like an airport here, like he says.

Silence.

NICK: Christ! (*He smiles.*) And I thought she was almost normal at first.

CHARLOTTE (*turns*): What?

NICK: She wasn't obviously cranky.

CHARLOTTE (*sharp*): Why should she be cranky. She's no more cranky than you or me.

NICK: I'm sorry. Of course all this is perfectly normal! The usual goings-on in the sun lounge! I suppose she's lonely.

CHARLOTTE: No. I don't think she's lonely. (*Matter of fact:*) There are a lot more people like her.

NICK: She *was* a little paranoid, wasn't she?

CHARLOTTE *has moved over to the radiator. Over the speakers we hear:* 'The coach to Preston has now left. The coach to Preston has now departed'.

NICK: There. She's gone anyway. One of your more extreme members I take it – is she?

CHARLOTTE (*by the radiator*): I don't know.

NICK (*sharp*): Why is she a member of two organisations?

CHARLOTTE: It's her choice.

NICK: Making sure she's fully covered for when the holocaust comes.

Pause.

Charlotte.

She turns.

You don't mind me calling you that I presume.

CHARLOTTE: It doesn't worry me, no.

NICK (*suddenly*): So you're the sort of conservation wing of the National Front . . . are you?

CHARLOTTE: No, we certainly are not!

NICK (*moving nearer her*): I mean the National Front's no joke anymore, Charlotte.

CHARLOTTE: Of course not. It never has been.

NICK: Are you connected with it in any way?

CHARLOTTE: No we are not! Why should we be? They're aware of our existence. But you're not really interested anyway.

NICK: Oh yes I am! Very! (*Getting near her:*) I mean where do you stand in all this, Charlotte?

CHARLOTTE (*facing him*): Stand in what?

NICK: I mean she was saying some pretty hideous things.

CHARLOTTE: She has her views . . . and I have mine.

NICK: And what are they?

CHARLOTTE: You know what they are. You read the leaflet.

NICK: I want to hear you say them. (*He grins.*) Explain them to me, Charlotte.

CHARLOTTE (*firm*): No. You'd only mock wouldn't you? (*She feels the radiator.*)

NICK: Is there anything there?

CHARLOTTE (*she feels very carefully then pulls her hand away suddenly*): I don't know – I don't think so.

NICK (*grins*): Of course not.

CHARLOTTE: Why of course?

NICK: She's the sort of person that thinks there are bombs and landmines in every litter bin, illegal immigrants everywhere, drugs in the lining of every car, isn't she? Why did you take that wire off her?

CHARLOTTE: I had to take it, didn't I?

She would have been offended otherwise. If it's no use we'll probably use it
for our Christmas decorations.

NICK (*smiles, amused*): I see!

CHARLOTTE: We can't get rid of you
here I suppose. You'd only go straight
down and sit in the van, wouldn't you?
You leave finally at Doncaster.

NICK: That's right. I promise.

KEVIN *enters, smiles at them.*

KEVIN: Ready? Ready to hit the high
road are you?

CHARLOTTE *moves away from
NICK.*

CHARLOTTE: Yes . . . we're ready.

Blackout

Scene Four

*Cinema posters and stills on one side of
the stage. Hot dog van in the middle. The
van is empty. The smell of onions.
Sausages piled up. Fanta orange machines
and Coke machines in the hot dog van. A
pocket television flickering at the side of
the van. Night. Stark lighting.
KEVIN and CHARLOTTE standing
waiting nervously.*

KEVIN: How long?

CHARLOTTE: He said ten o'clock. He
should be here very soon. (*She looks
about her.*) I don't even know what he
looks like, but he'll be here. (*She takes
out a handkerchief, wipes her face.*)

KEVIN: This is the right place, is it?
You've looked on the list?

CHARLOTTE (*sharp*): I told you, yes.

KEVIN: You all right, Charlotte?

CHARLOTTE: Yes, I'm fine. I could
have done without the company we
had on the journey.

KEVIN: Nick?

CHARLOTTE: Yes, we've done very
well otherwise, haven't we? We're
ahead of schedule. (*Pause. She glances

around.) I just feel a little exposed
standing out here.

KEVIN *drinks from a wine bottle.*

Don't drink too much, Kevin.

KEVIN: No, of coure not. (*He takes
another drink, nervously rubs hand
across the wall.*) It's pretty filthy
round here isn't it?

A police siren in the distance.

KEVIN (*flicks round*): What's that?

CHARLOTTE: It's all right – (*But she
tenses slightly too.*) I saw a fire engine
dash up a street in London not so long
ago. It was two, three in the morning.
All the streets were deserted, but it
was roaring up them, screaming its
head off, its siren was screaming. It
came to this square, and started going
round and round in circles, making
this extraordinary noise. I think they
were just having a bit of fun, trying to
wake people up. But nobody stirred.
Nobody shouted. Nobody moved at
all.

NICK *enters, CHARLOTTE looks up
in surprise.*

CHARLOTTE: What?

NICK *stares at her, slight smile.*

CHARLOTTE: Why are you here?

NICK: I followed you.

CHARLOTTE: So I see. Why?

NICK: I don't know really. Just an
impulse, an instinct, I hope you don't
mind.

CHARLOTTE: We *had said goodbye.*

NICK: I know.

KEVIN: Yes, we had Nick.

CHARLOTTE: You don't intend to
stay here I hope.

NICK: What? (*Worried by the tension in
the air:*) I thought you'd be pleased to
see me. (*Pause.*) What's happening
here anyway?

KEVIN (*suddenly looks up*): Yes, where
is he?

NICK: Who? (*He turns, stares at

CHARLOTTE.) Who you waiting for Charlotte?

CHARLOTTE: We're just . . . waiting for someone, that's all.

NICK: Who? (*He stares at the hot dog stand.*) Not him? (*He looks at the hot dog stand.*) The little man from behind here?

CHARLOTTE (*very quiet, controlled nerves*): We're waiting . . . for a hamburger.

KEVIN: See here – it's just closed down.

NICK (*swings round nervously*): What?

KEVIN: The cinema! Last week – it's closed down, it's finished.

NICK (*swings back again*): The hot dog man. You're waiting for the hot dog man!

CHARLOTTE (*very quiet*): I didn't say that.

NICK (*excited*): I don't believe it. I can't believe it! You mean he! (*He points.*) Him! The guy who stuffs sausages into these. (*He holds up a fistful of onions.*) He's *one* of you – is he?

CHARLOTTE (*very quiet*): Is he what?

NICK (*shouts*): One of you? A member. Another member!

She is sitting on a step, completely still. No reply.

(NICK *smiles.*) He is? (*Moving round:*) And you've come to collect off him – have you?

Pause.

What's he going to give you?

CHARLOTTE (*very quiet*): That's our business, I think.

NICK (*delighted*): So he is going to give you something. (*Loud.*) Come on! What you going to get off him? (*Fast.*) What secret goodies is he bringing? What's he bringing?

KEVIN: Same as before.

NICK (*swings round*): Same as before. I see. Then why you so nervous?

CHARLOTTE: Nervous?

KEVIN (*trying to lessen the tension*): Here, want a fag? Help you calm down. (*He gives him a cigarette.*) When I start rolling one – I like rolling seven or eight.

NICK: You're not going to get arms off him are you, Charlotte?

CHARLOTTE *remains still.*

CHARLOTTE (*puzzled tone, quiet*): Arms?

NICK (*smiling, mocking*): I mean he's not . . . (*He laughs.*) he is not going to produce a few grenades out of the sausages and hand them over 15 pence a time. Do they come with onions, or do you go out to a dark country lane with him and get them there. (*He moves over to the hamburger stand, stares at it.*) Fortunately for you, I don't believe it's possible. I mean that is just a little too unlikely, just a tiny bit too fantastic. I mean it's been a strange day, but not that strange.

CHARLOTTE: Please, just go.

NICK *flicks through the buns on the stall.*

NICK: Is it just from this one charming little stall or will any do – are there hundreds dotted over everywhere, the whole country?

Silence.

(*Loud.*) Charlotte? (*With nervous energy, trying to get a reaction.*) I mean, the terrible thing about grenades these days is they all come covered with tomato juice and mustard already on them, whether you like it or not, not like the good old English grenade. I mean there's absolutely no freedom of choice anymore is there? You can go into a nice ordinary hamburger house – can I have a grenade please, and it comes in fifteen seconds, totally packaged in this nasty box, and smothered in all kinds of filth, hardly recognisable. It's the terrible American influence isn't it?

Silence.

(*Aggressive.*) Not funny? NO.

Silence.

KEVIN: You realise we're in the middle.

NICK: Middle of what?

KEVIN: Middle of England. Middle of Britain. The heart as it were. We're standing on it. Now!

NICK (*ignoring him, looking at* CHARLOTTE): Isn't this all a trifle dangerous for you, out in the open air?

CHARLOTTE (*calmly but strongly*): Why don't you just go, Nick? Leave us alone.

NICK: No, I'm keeping you company aren't I? (*He smiles.*) I'm here to stay.

CHARLOTTE *looks away.*

KEVIN: I'm very thirsty now.

NICK: Why don't you help yourself. (*He indicates the hamburger stand.*)

CHARLOTTE: No, that would be breaking the law, wouldn't it.

NICK (*smiles, mocking*): Of course! The law. You're completely law-abiding, I forgot.

CHARLOTTE: Yes, of course.

NICK (*loud*): Why's Kevin so nervous then?

KEVIN: I'm not nervous. Not at all . . . (*Staring at a poster.*) There's the last poster see, for the cinema, already fading fast.

NICK (*reading, smiling*): 'The Killer Elite'.

KEVIN: Yeah. We can't even keep our cinemas open anymore, in this country, can we? Used to be the centre of the community didn't it? No British movies anymore, nothing really.

NICK (*in a teasing tone*): Are you a movie freak then, Kevin?

CHARLOTTE: Do you have to shout all the time?

KEVIN: Just a bit. You see my eyes have a little difficulty, as you may have noticed. I'm probably going blind.

NICK (*stunned, only half believing*): Blind?

KEVIN: No, don't worry – I've got a disease up here, in these orbs. No real stopping it.

NICK: I'm sorry. I didn't realise.

KEVIN: No need to be. Doesn't worry me.

NICK: That explains a lot.

CHARLOTTE: I thought you'd make a remark like that.

KEVIN: So I went to the movies. I saw everything that they poured out. I went twice a day when I could afford it.

NICK: You should get them on the National Health, shouldn't you? The movies, I mean.

KEVIN: No, I've stopped going. Didn't want to take any more.

NICK (*loud*): So you've been living off films have you, Kevin?

KEVIN: That's right. Me and a few others. Hey! Imagine going in there now, into the empty cinema, there's a whole cinema there behind us, just waiting, with a bare screen, probably going brown now, being chewed up. Imagine going in there now.

NICK: Yes! Why not.

KEVIN: And you could sit me down, my head's full of pictures you see, you could sit me down, point me straight at the screen, give me one small hit on the head, or something like that, and we'd be away. I could pour it out onto the screen. All of it! Onto that empty screen. All that I've seen.

NICK: Yes, you could, Kevin.

KEVIN: No, I mean it. I've seen it all. Seen some great skin pictures.

NICK: Yes, you must have seen some pretty dirty things.

CHARLOTTE (*warning*): Kevin . . .

KEVIN: Yeah – I've seen some really filthy things, yeah and also some pretty weird ones, oh yes, spikes, big spikes, on metal gloves, and all over cars, and on people's tongues, yes! Saw a few forests, that was nice, and a few deserts, one all covered in tar, and a lot of needles too – (*He grins.*) – they all run into each other, you see! Yes! And some pretty, you know, unpleasant things too, heads split open, running free.

NICK: Really?

KEVIN: And killings. Hundreds of killings, of course. In different colours, different ways, fast and slow, falling past you, and women's feet in bear traps. (*Loud.*) Yeah! There these car thieves, you see, a big gang, they steal cars and smash them up, in America, and blow them up all over the city. They wear stocking masks. Yes! And they always go back to this one great car park at night, forty stories high! And the police can't catch them, so this head guard, he puts down man-traps in the dark, he does! And this girl's leg goes into the metal man-trap, and it's bitten off her, the teeth goes in, and it bites it off, (*He flicks his hand.*) just like that! YOU SEE IT.

CHARLOTTE: Kevin . . .

KEVIN (*carrying straight on, fast, louder and louder*): And the head guard, he's got a withered arm – from Vietnam – with steel finger-nails – and he goes mad, you see, to catch this gang, and he goes round all the traps at dawn, collecting the feet in each one, he has a sackful of feet. *You see them!* Squashed in together, in a pile.

NICK *is grinning, drinking, watching* KEVIN.

CHARLOTTE: Please, Kevin, I don't want to hear . . .

KEVIN (*carrying straight on – oblivious, loud, fast*): And he hangs them above his bed, the feet! From his mantel-piece. You see them on this kitchen wire, dangling there, he plays with them! They stay there the whole film going bad. Slowly. They do!

NICK (*loud, grinning*): *All right, Kevin!* We get the . . .

KEVIN (*carrying straight on*): And he gets caught in *one of his own traps* at the end, because he's put down so many, hundreds! And he tears himself

out, and *it really hurts him!* You see it! It's *not nice.* And he crawls over the whole town with one leg, on his belly along the pavement, with a machine-gun, hunting them across these concrete walls, and across bridges, you see him crawling, and leaving a trail of blood and things behind him . . .

CHARLOTTE: Kevin, please, sssh.

KEVIN (*really loud*): And he gets face to face with the leader of the gang, and he blows his head off, and its bursts open, it bursts right open, splashes over all of them!

NICK (*grins*): Kevin, stop!

KEVIN (*very loud*): Then the rest of the gang get HIM, the guard, and they throw him into a dust-cart shredder, you know, and he's squashed, and eaten, and shredded up, you know, by the spikes, screaming his head off, screaming so loudly, really loudly, and they pick up little raw bits of him, they do, collect him in their hands. (*He screams.*) RAW PIECES OF HIM. YOU SAW IT.

Pause.

You see! (*Quieter.*) *That's* the last movie I saw, it's just run through my head, *unfortunately.*

NICK: Not very nice, no!

KEVIN: Could see how mad they were getting. Weirder and weirder. You began to feel a bit funny down here – (*He feels his stomach.*) – in your insides, as you went into the dark, before it started.

NICK: Did you, Kevin? You shouldn't have gone then . . .

KEVIN: Mad, mad images, they reflect things more than you imagine. Oh yes! You can see what's happening all right in the world, if you think, *if you really think about what you've seen*, when you come out of the dark, the attitudes in it, the sort of madness, you can see the whole sickness.

NICK (*loud*): No, you can't. They're only films, Kevin – *just films*, and they release things in some people.

KEVIN: No! No! I ought to run them for you now, while we wait, then you'll see. *Give a free show.*

NICK: OK then! Yes! Run them for me, now. Give me a playback. Run them now . . .

KEVIN (*grins*): No, sorry, no, I'm talking shit.

CHARLOTTE: Calm down both of you, that's enough.

NICK: No come on, run them for me . . . . . come on! You said you would! Splash them all over the walls of Doncaster.

CHARLOTTE: Stop it!

NICK (*pulling* KEVIN – *excited*): There's a wall. That one. About the size of a screen. It'll do perfectly.

KEVIN: No, look I'm talking shit, forget it. (*Loud.*) I mean how can I run them on that *wall*, it's absurd, isn't it?

NICK (*very animated*): No, run them, come on, I want to see.

CHARLOTTE: Just ignore him, Kevin.

KEVIN: No, look it was terrible shit. Forget I spoke.

NICK (*loud*): No! Kevin . . .

KEVIN: Always the best policy.

NICK (*pulling him up*): Come on do it! Run them. Let's see it Kevin! Do you want me to start it! (*He points* KEVIN's *head straight ahead. Very loud:*) There! Right *Kevin*. Run them, now. (*Even louder:*) NOW!

KEVIN (*standing facing the wall, standing very straight, arms by his side*): OK then . . . if you *really* want it.

CHARLOTTE: Just leave him alone, you've got him drunk.

KEVIN: No, he hasn't. (*He takes off his dark glasses; slight smile, then loud:*) A lot of strange muck will come out, of course. Here goes then! (*His arm stiffens by his side – slight pause.*) My eyes should light up, shouldn't they really, and film come out of my ears

and round into my mouth for the full effect. (*He stiffens.*) Here it comes then! (*He stands very straight, eyes wide, a noise like a projector beginning to come out of him, which turns into a high-pitched whine, which grows louder and louder, and really piercing.*)

NICK (*suddenly breaking away*): You're both completely crazy, do you know that? Complete nuts, look at you, a freak and an overgrown schoolgirl on this ludicrous trip through England! One of you thinks you're a film projector –

KEVIN: That's only a joke, mate . . .

NICK (*carrying straight on*): The other sits by a hot dog stand, expecting it to cough up rifles. (*He smiles.*) You're both completely gone – fortunately for the rest of us. Just a couple of little cranks.

CHARLOTTE: You're very drunk too, aren't you? Far too drunk.

NICK: Am I? (*He moves away.*) Oh no, I'm not. (*Moving further away.*) You realise of course I could expose the whole organisation now if I wanted, the whole tiny network, the whole cobweb of shabby semi-fascist study groups, little grubby fanatics whispering about England in corners. Could expose the lot if I wanted. Couldn't I? 'Bye now. I've got to piss. Nice knowing you – or was it? (*About to go:*) But I may be back. (*He goes.*)

The stage cross-fades to semi-darkness, the sound of urinals flushing, sputter of water. Lavatory atmosphere, although all we see is NICK *in the half light, back to the audience, relieving himself.*
For a moment he's alone, shaking his head slightly. CHARLOTTE *enters behind him.*

CHARLOTTE: Are you there?

NICK *turns.*

NICK: You shouldn't be in a Gentlemen's lavatory –

CHARLOTTE: But I am – there's nobody about anyway.

NICK: Yes – why is that? (*He swings round.*) Why is the whole fucking place deserted. The hot dog stand, the urinals, it's a fucking ghost town, the whole place has stopped breathing. Where is everybody?

CHARLOTTE (*staring straight at him*): They're all indoors watching television probably. (*At him:*) Aren't they?

NICK: Except you two! It's very dark, Charlotte – isn't it?

CHARLOTTE: I'm sure it's meant to be closed, Nick. It's hot even here!

Pause. CHARLOTTE *is looking at him.*

NICK: You know I haven't seen you sweat yet.

CHARLOTTE: Haven't you? (*She looks over her shoulder.*) I ought to spend a penny myself actually.

NICK (*amused smile*): Spend a penny?

CHARLOTTE: That's right, yes.

CHARLOTTE *moves into darkness, suddenly she stops, having trodden on something. She stoops, picks up smashed toy, an 'action man' model, mangled, its head battered, filthy, pushed into a hole in the floor.*

CHARLOTTE (*to herself*): Look at that.

The sound of cisterns flushing in the darkness.

NICK: Yes!

CHARLOTTE (*handling it carefully*): It's very dirty! Who would have done that, mangled it? Children I suppose, fighting. The savagery of what they do – it's torn to pieces.

NICK: It's not savagery at all – just energy.

CHARLOTTE (*turning*): How can you possibly know?

NICK: Because I do!

Pause.

Because I'm good with kids believe it or not.

Pause.

Which you won't! It's what I like doing actually, playgrounds, community projects, (*Defiant.*) that sort of thing, Charlotte!

CHARLOTTE *glances into shadows.*

What? Nobody? Some people probably still feel forced to meet here – leaving messages on walls.

CHARLOTTE: They're worse than rats those sort of people. (*She drops the model onto the floor.*)

NICK (*disbelief*): What did you say . . . ?

CHARLOTTE: They're worse than . . .

NICK: Yes, I heard. Extraordinary thing to say. Come here Charlotte. (*He catches hold of her arms; the cisterns flush.*) They flush a lot those cisterns. Perhaps they've gone mad like everything else tonight, can't stop flushing. (*Up close to her:*) Do you think there's somebody in one of the cubicles now, a special sort of fascist dwarf, that comes out at night, never sees daylight at all, comes out when it catches your scent, when it knows you're in town. (*Aggressive.*) We are not amused are we? (*Loud, confident.*) You're unnerving me, Charlotte!

CHARLOTTE: Am I? You've been drinking too much.

NICK: No I haven't.

CHARLOTTE: I've come to tell you I want you to be on your way.

NICK: Yes. (*He smiles.*) Yes!

CHARLOTTE: I mean it.

NICK: Of course you do.

CHARLOTTE: Right.

She moves to try to go, but he blocks her, moves in on her.

NICK: I'm not sure about you, Charlotte, you know.

CHARLOTTE: Aren't you? Why not?

NICK (*smiles*): I mean, I can understand about Kevin thinking like he does. I mean, he's one of those sixties' left-overs, isn't he really, a great many of them about at the moment, an epidemic, I meet them everywhere. Lost in his own pool of exciting memories isn't he? Especially when summer comes. I mean, he's quite a nice guy in his way, with his eyes and all his movies. Got some imagination too, hasn't he, a spark . . . It's just a little unfortunate isn't it, when the Easy Rider bit goes badly sour, a little sad. He's just a crank now.

CHARLOTTE (*turning on him*): He *is not* a crank. I have told you. No more than you, probably considerably less. Why do people always have to be cranky to feel things strongly? (*She moves.*) Now can I get out.

NICK (*barring her way, smiling*): Yes! But you Charlotte, you're not quite so simple are you?

CHARLOTTE: Kevin's not simple. Can I . . . ?

NICK (*ignoring her*): I mean, most extreme right wing *cranks*, I mean the actual activists, are usually bandy-legged little tin soldiers, isn't that right? You know those typical slightly manic faces, the pictures of them, their eyes staring out at you, full of the usual English sort of hatreds, Charlotte, (*Watching her closely.*) foreigners . . . sex . . . change, all that, desperately trying to whip it all up now. (*Loud.*) Right? You can recognise them a mile off; *I know*. We used to live near one of them when I was a kid, who's now quite famous, he used to sing to himself, in the street when he saw somebody coloured. Yes sing! 'Black Beetle, Black Beetle, stick him with a needle'. He did. Not loudly. But you could hear him.

CHARLOTTE: They're pathetic nonentities.

NICK: Who?

CHARLOTTE: The leaders of the National Front. They're ridiculous . . . useless.

The lavatories flush.

NICK (*up close to her*): But I mean you, Charlotte, you're not bandy-legged,

are you?

CHARLOTTE: No?

NICK: At least it doesn't appear so, or balding. (*He smiles.*) I mean, you probably approach being a normal healthy girl. Quite attractive in a schoolmistressy, English-rose sort of way. You don't seem to be suffering from a hatred of your body, disgust at the bodily functions.

CHARLOTTE (*quiet*): No . . . I'm not.

NICK: Probably enjoy an energetic screw as much as most people.

CHARLOTTE: Sometimes, yes . . . with the right person.

NICK (*suddenly up to her, loud*): So what do you really believe in, Charlotte? (*Urgent:*) Come on. What?

CHARLOTTE: I told you, it's in the leaflet. That's all you need to know. (*By him.*) *I want you to leave.*

NICK (*smiles*): I am.

CHARLOTTE: Good.

CHARLOTTE *moves as if relieved,* NICK *suddenly catches her.*

NICK: But first, Charlotte. Come here. (*He pulls her close – quite roughly.*) We're in an underground toilet, in the middle of Doncaster, the entire population is watching telly, there is an abandoned hot dog stand outside – and you're going to tell me all the *rest's a joke.*

CHARLOTTE *stares.*

Hamburgers and arms.

CHARLOTTE: You mentioned those, didn't you?

NICK: I know.

Pause.

CHARLOTTE: All the rest's a bit of a joke, yes. (*She smiles very slightly.*)

NICK: That's better. At last! (*He is still barring her way.*) You're all goose-pimply suddenly. (*He touches her off-handedly.*)

CHARLOTTE: That's because I don't particularly like being touched by you.

NICK: No, of course not.

CHARLOTTE: Like all stupid people, you're very clumsy, aren't you?

The cisterns flush.

I don't like men's lavatories very much, they must be the ugliest places in the world. But that's quite appropriate isn't it? (*She touches his crotch in a detached way.*)

NICK: Yes, Charlotte. (*He grins.*) That's right.

CHARLOTTE (*moving her hand away*): Just think if there was a whole mass consisting of holes like these, suddenly there they were, they'd grown up, side by side, back to back, like all those screaming echoing subways you walk through at night. If you woke up in the morning, and that's all there was everywhere . . . everywhere you breathed was *like this* stench, tasted like this.

NICK (*loud*): But that's not what everything's like, (*Aggressive:*) is it?

CHARLOTTE: What would you do, Nick?

NICK: If it happened, I'd get out.

CHARLOTTE: No, you wouldn't, because there's nowhere to go.

NICK (*amused smile*): No, of course not, nowhere.

CHARLOTTE (*suddenly loud*): There isn't.

NICK (*grins*): No.

CHARLOTTE: That's right, that's better.

NICK (*amused smile*): Yes, Charlotte. (*He touches her again.*) The goose-pimples have gone now, almost a throb going through you.

CHARLOTTE: Is there? . . . Yes. (*Suddenly she turns.*) No. I've had enough now. It's time to get back to work. (*She moves.*) Can I . . . ? (*She brushes past him and out.*)

Lights up on the whole stage. The hamburger van, KEVIN sitting there.

NICK (*suddenly mocking, excited tone*):

Nobody's come? See!

KEVIN: No.

CHARLOTTE: Have you been watching?

NICK: Of course he has.

KEVIN: Yes.

CHARLOTTE (*sharp*): *Have* you been watching?

KEVIN: Yes, Charlotte . . . I told you, been watching everything.

NICK: What he can see, that is.

CHARLOTTE (*quiet*): Why isn't he here?

NICK: Why indeed?

CHARLOTTE (*turns on him*): You're going now, Nick . . . NOW!

NICK (*grins*): In a moment, not now. I want to see how long you're going to keep this up. It's getting late you know. Are you going to camp on the building-site over there then Charlotte? Among the scaffolding and the cement-mixers. Not quite what you're used to, is it? Or maybe inside Kevin's rotting cinema. Pitch your tent in the middle of that.

CHARLOTTE: I told you. Just go.

KEVIN: I'm thirsty anyway. (*He gets up and looks towards the hamburger van.*)

CHARLOTTE: I told you not to touch that . . . it's against the law.

NICK: She must be joking, Kevin – mustn't she? Who on earth's going to know?

KEVIN: Yes. (*Looking at the van.*)

CHARLOTTE: I told you not to.

KEVIN: But I've got to drink something in this heat.

CHARLOTTE: You've drunk enough.

NICK: Come on, let's defy her shall we, Kevin?

They suddenly rush over to the van.

How do we get in? (*He pulls the door open.*)

KEVIN (*pulls at the lever of the Fanta*

machine): This doesn't work!

NICK: It must work.

CHARLOTTE: You're being immensely stupid.

KEVIN: Give them a good pull.

NICK: Pull! Pull! Tiny trickle out of this one! Come on. Like milking a metal cow isn't it?

KEVIN (*taking the lid off*): Only onion-flavoured water in here – can pour that out. Packet of uncooked sausages. (*He tosses them onto the ground.*) No good to us. (*He suddenly splashes the onion water out – great splashes.*)

KEVIN: Come on get it!

The whole van begins to shake violently; NICK is tugging on the handle.

NICK: It's coming! Coming!

CHARLOTTE: *Stop it . . .*

TAYLOR, *a young police constable, enters. They all look up.*

TAYLOR: All right – let's have you over here.

They stand still.

I said let's have you out here, over here.

NICK (*smiles*): That would happen, wouldn't it? (*He doesn't notice CHARLOTTE's tense face.*)

TAYLOR (*to NICK*): What were you doing with that machine?

CHARLOTTE (*sharp*): They were just getting a drink.

TAYLOR (*glances at CHARLOTTE*): I was speaking to the gentlemen. (*To NICK and KEVIN:*) Helping yourself, were you, that the idea? All right. (*He takes out his notebook.*)

NICK: He's very young, isn't he? Do you realise he's probably younger than me?

TAYLOR: You all together, you three?

NICK: No.

CHARLOTTE: Yes, we are.

TAYLOR (*looking at them*): So you're all together. What were you doing out here anyway?

KEVIN: Waiting . . .

TAYLOR: Waiting for what? (*Pause.*) All right. (*To KEVIN:*) Could you open that bag please – (*He turns to CHARLOTTE.*) – and yours too.

CHARLOTTE: Why?

TAYLOR: Open that bag please – routine check.

NICK (*grins*): He's sweating – it's a very thick uniform.

TAYLOR: Come on, I haven't got all night. I've got a bed to go to, let's have those bags open.

KEVIN *lowers his bag, opens it to show inside. TAYLOR moves across to it. CHARLOTTE shoots him from a gun in her handbag. Very loud explosion. He fells on his face. NICK makes a noise of spontaneous shock as the explosion happens. CHARLOTTE crosses over to TAYLOR, stands by him for a moment, her dress brushing his body. She empties the gun into him. Silence. Fast fade down. On the soundtrack: a loud electric buzz lasting 50 seconds in the blackout.*

End of Act One

ACT TWO

Scene One

The noise heard at end of Act One returns at full volume.
After 10 seconds of this an explosion of bright neon light. The motorway cafe, stark, dirty, very late at night. The neons are overpowering.
KEVIN, NICK and CHARLOTTE are standing at the edge of the cafe area, with NICK in the middle of the three.
Upstage there's a trolley laden with food remains and dirty plates. The WOMAN CLEANER, about 34, overtired bedraggled appearance, is stacking plates on the trolley, back to audience, seemingly oblivious of the three of them. They stand there, for a split second, a still moment as CHARLOTTE glances over the tables. KEVIN lifts a milk bottle that he's holding, throws back his head, takes a long drink, wipes his mouth.
CHARLOTTE glances towards the CLEANER, who glances back at her then away. KEVIN takes another drink of milk.

CHARLOTTE (*moving down to one of the tables*): Here'll do. Come on.

KEVIN (*not moving*): What?

CHARLOTTE: Here. (*She puts her handbag on the table, the carrier bag by the chair.*) That's better. Sit down Nick – there.

NICK moves slowly, but obediently sits opposite her.

NICK (*quiet*): Yes.

KEVIN (*very quiet, also sits slowly, glancing round him*): There's a comb in this ashtray. (*He pulls the ashtray towards him.*) See, there's a comb here. (*He drinks out of the milk bottle.*)

CHARLOTTE: Can I. (*She takes the milk bottle; keeping her eye very firmly on NICK and her handbag out of reach, she takes a long drink of milk.*)

KEVIN (*indicating milk*): It's very warm I'm afraid. (*Nervous.*) It's almost bubbling.

CHARLOTTE: Yes. (*She holds out the milk bottle to NICK.*) Do you want some?

NICK: No. (*Very quiet.*) No I don't.

CHARLOTTE: Sure? Then would you pass one of those. The napkins.

She is pointing to the paper napkins – NICK moves slowly.

(*Sharp.*) Come on. (*He passes them – she wipes her mouth.*) We've got to get something to eat quickly. We have to fetch it.

KEVIN (*glancing up*): We're high up here. Can keep a watch out. The light's very bright isn't it. You can't look straight at them at all can you. Can't we . . .

CHARLOTTE (*firm*): Kevin . . . sssshh!

The CLEANER comes up to the table. KEVIN tenses.

CLEANER (*slight smile*): It's hot tonight isn't it?

KEVIN (*sharp*): Yes it is.

CLEANER: So what you going to have?

They look up.

I'm not meant to serve you as you know, but it makes a change. So what do you want? Plaice and chips. Chicken Maryland. The Chicken Maryland's not bad.

CHARLOTTE (*sharp*): Thank you – that's kind of you. (*She looks at the men.*) We've got to eat. We'll have three Chicken Marylands.

NICK: Not for me. (*He looks up.*) I don't want any Charlotte.

CHARLOTTE: He'll have a coffee then.

KEVIN: And some milk . . . can we have some more milk.

CLEANER (*smiles*): I better get that down. Do it properly. (*She takes a napkin off the table, and a pen out of the pocket in her tunic. She tries to write.*) It doesn't work! (*She wets the tip of the pen.*) It's not writing.

KEVIN (*loud*): It's all right, we can get it . . . *We'll* get it now!

CLEANER: No. I'll remember it. Two Marylands, coffee, glass of milk.

KEVIN: No, could we – I want a jug of milk. (*He glances at* CHARLOTTE.) A jug – a large jug. (*Loud.*) And it's got to be cold, ice cold.

CLEANER (*hesitating*): I don't know if there is a jug here.

CHARLOTTE: If you're going to fetch our food – could we have it *very quickly.*

CLEANER (*surprised*): Yes – it's over there already. It's just lying there. (*She moves off.*)

Silence.

KEVIN (*glances over his shoulder*): We ought to have gone and got it – ourselves.

CHARLOTTE: No. (*She looks at* NICK.) You should have something to eat.

NICK (*looks up, very quiet*): Should I?

CHARLOTTE (*forceful*): Yes, you should.

NICK (*very quiet*): Of course.

Silence – they sit still.

KEVIN (*suddenly loud*): How long do we have to sit here – under these lights here.

CHARLOTTE: Not long.

KEVIN (*fast words tumbling out*): Be a great place for a film too – wouldn't it. Chickens slowly going round on their spits . . . in their lockers.

CHARLOTTE (*tense*): It's all right, Kevin.

KEVIN: See them, behind glass getting brown slowly. Could have other things going round – cats.

Pause.

Don't know why I said that.

The CLEANER *enters with a tray of food.*

CLEANER: There you are. Two Mary-lands, *jug* of milk.

KEVIN *takes the jug of milk immediately, and drinks out of it, large gulping drink.*

You're very thirsty aren't you?

KEVIN: Yes! (*He holds jug, feeling the cold.*) I am.

CLEANER (*she stands by table – smiles.*) You going far?

CHARLOTTE (*looks up*): Yes, we are, quite a way.

The television noise dips.

CLEANER (*picking up a paper napkin from the table, folding it*): We're not that busy tonight. (*She smiles – slowly.*) My husband comes out here sometimes. Occasionally. Suddenly you look up, and there he is; you get the shock of your life. But he can only come out a very few nights. It's a quite way you see.

CHARLOTTE: Yes, I see. How much do we owe you?

CLEANER: You can't pay me – you pay over there.

CHARLOTTE (*sharp*): I want to pay now – I'm going to pay you.

CLEANER (*slight smile.*) Could get sacked for that.

CHARLOTTE: How much?

CLEANER: Two pounds thirty.

KEVIN (*tense*): Right. We'll give you the money.

CLEANER (*standing at the table – just as* CHARLOTTE *gets out her purse*): It gets busier again later. Right in the early hours. You get some funny types then.

CHARLOTTE (*getting the money out of her purse*): I'm sure.

CLEANER (*carrying straight on*): Few nights ago this lorry driver came in, I looked up and there he was standing just over there – (*She indicates.*) – and he had – (*She laughs.*) – his trousers were round his ankles, no I swear it, right round his ankles, and his pants – (*She laughs.*) – they were down too, right down, I swear, he was standing just here.

CHARLOTTE (*holding money, getting tense*): Yes, I see.

CLEANER: He was so drunk, he couldn't see a foot in front of him and he sat down, sort of singing quiet to himself, he had a high voice, and all the time he was doing it down his leg . . . you know. He was quite good-looking you know, but he couldn't really move at all.

CHARLOTTE: Yes. Here's the money.

KEVIN: OK.

CLEANER: Yes. (*She takes the money, holds it in her hand.*) Where do you come from?

CHARLOTTE: We've come from London . . .

CLEANER: I come from round here. I can remember when the road was being built – yes – I saw it being dug out, watched it. And I walked along it before it was open too. Yes. Right down the middle – where all that is moving now. (*She indicates the traffic.*)

NICK (*quiet, looking straight at CHARLOTTE*): I don't feel very well, I think . . .

CHARLOTTE (*staring straight back at him*): Then you better eat something – here. (*She pulls a bit of food off her plate.*)

NICK (*a little louder*): I don't want to eat.

CLEANER: Do you want me to get you anything else?

CHARLOTTE (*really terse*): No, thank you. We're all right now . . .

CLEANER (*smiles at them, wiping the corner of the table automatically as she talks*): It's funny you know, people look at you in here, they're amazed you can talk; you should see the surpise on their faces, that you *can* actually tell them things, yes, that there's something going on in your

head after all.

KEVIN (*beginning to get extraordinarily tense*): Right, I see. It must be . . .

CLEANER (*carrying on, smiling to herself*): Not all of them of course, you know, the Army come through here one night – some soldiers, going somewhere in a truck. They livened things up all right. They were very young, about ten of them you see. Jumping all round here, on the tables. Sent us all mad. It was about a couple of months ago now . . .

KEVIN (*bursting out*): OK. Could you just leave us now. All right. (*Pause.*) Thanks, but could you go . . . Right, sorry – but we're in a hurry.

CHARLOTTE (*watching her*): Yes.

CLEANER: Yes. (*She stares back at them.*) I've got to go to the kitchens now anyway.

She goes. CHARLOTTE *stares at the food.*

CHARLOTTE: OK – just eat now. (*To NICK:*) Drink your coffee. (*She turns the Chicken Maryland round on her plate.*) I'm going to take all the batter off this . . . scrape it off.

She does so. Silence.

NICK (*picks up his coffee – then puts it down staring at her*): Look – you're eating it.

CHARLOTTE (*looking up*): What?

NICK: You're eating it – see. (*Pause.*) See – she's . . .

CHARLOTTE: Yes. (*She puts the piece down, her face tense.*) But it doesn't taste of anything. You ought to eat too,' I told you . . . (*She suddenly turns to KEVIN's plate.*) Mind Kevin, there's something in yours – (*She picks at it.*) A hair, I think . . .

NICK (*still staring straight at CHARLOTTE, fiddling with the sugar bowl*): You know she – (*He looks down at the table – stirring the sugar round.*) You know Charlotte's got blood all down her dress don't you . . .

CHARLOTTE *continues to eat – she doesn't look at him.*

Do you realise she's sitting there with it down her, all down that side.

CHARLOTTE (*suddenly looks up*): Don't do that Nick (*Tense, pale.*) Please . . .

NICK: You can feel it. You can feel it under the table.

CHARLOTTE (*looking straight at him*): Can you?

NICK (*quieter*): Yes.

She takes a napkin, picks up her chicken leg.

CHARLOTTE: I'm keeping this for later. I didn't particularly want anything fried. (*She gets up.*) I'm going to change. (*She hands KEVIN her handbag.*) Just finish your food. I'll be back very quickly. (*She moves towards the exit.*)

NICK (*suddenly calls out in a very loud voice, ringing out over whole cafeteria*): CHARLOTTE? . . . WHERE'S CHARLOTTE GOING – WHERE'S SHE GOING?

CHARLOTTE *stops, turns. Pause.*

(*Still shouting.*) What's she going to do . . .

CHARLOTTE (*clenched*): Stop it, Nick.

NICK (*still loud*): Where's Charlotte going . . . ?

Silence. CHARLOTTE crosses back to the table, right up to NICK.

CHARLOTTE (*clipped, right by NICK*): You better both come out too then, hadn't you.

Cross fade to the foyer.
The same powerful neon lighting.
Amusement machines lined up – 'On Safari' (shooting at elephants). Distant music seeping through speakers, litter on the floor.
They enter. CHARLOTTE moves across the foyer.

CHARLOTTE: Kevin – stay here with him.

KEVIN (*mechanically*): Stay here with him.

CHARLOTTE: Yes. (*She moves to go.*)

NICK (*loud*): Charlotte!

CHARLOTTE *turns.*

CHARLOTTE: I'm just going to change.

NICK *suddenly crosses the foyer, presses right up to her by a machine.*

NICK (*nervous, hostile*): Going to change out of your working clothes then . . . ?

KEVIN (*coming up close*): Leave her –

CHARLOTTE (*up against the machine*): Nick . . . Stop it.

KEVIN (*moving up, takes NICK's arm*): Leave off her mate . . . don't try . . .

NICK: Going to change?

CHARLOTTE: Yes.

NICK: It's wet. (*His arm touches the side of her dress.*)

KEVIN: I told you – leave her alone. (*He pulls him off forcibly.*) Come on . . .

KEVIN *holds NICK. CHARLOTTE stares at NICK across the foyer.*

CHARLOTTE: You were hurting me.

NICK (*loud*): Was I?

KEVIN: Sssssh!

CHARLOTTE: Leave this to me – it's all right.

NICK (*still loud, staring across at CHARLOTTE's dress*): Could feel it down the back of your leg –

CHARLOTTE (*steely*): Just calm down, Nick.

KEVIN: Charlotte – shall I . . .

CHARLOTTE: No, Kevin – it's all right. (*Staring straight at NICK's eyes:*) You're going to control yourself, Nick . . .

NICK (*loud*): That's right!

CHARLOTTE (*dangerous*): Do you understand me?

NICK: Yes.

Pause.

(*He suddenly shouts.*) I am nothing to do with these two. I have nothing . . .

KEVIN (*loud, jumps*): Stop it! Just stop it. We're armed, you know.

Pause.

CHARLOTTE (*her tone slightly gentler*): Don't raise your voice again.

NICK (*his arm held by* KEVIN – *staring at* CHARLOTTE): I'm going now.

CHARLOTTE: You can't.

KEVIN: Listen, mate . . .

CHARLOTTE (*cutting in*): You're not going anywhere. I've already told you. You're staying with us and doing what you're told. And then it'll be all right. You're safer with us.

NICK (*quieter, bit defiant*): Yes.

KEVIN (*still*): Where would you go anyway?

NICK (*totally bewildered*): What do you mean where would I go?

KEVIN: *Where* would you go? It's hundreds of yards to the road. There's nowhere to go – see.

NICK (*glances up*): Yes.

They watch him.

CHARLOTTE (*firm*): Now control yourself.

NICK: Yes. (*For a split second he looks at her; then suddenly:*) Shall we go into the shop? (*Louder.*) We'll go into the souvenir shop, shall we?

CHARLOTTE (*very steely*): It's closed.

NICK: I want to buy something. OK. You going to stop me, Charlotte?

CHARLOTTE (*staring straight at him*): It's closed, Nick.

NICK (*trying to raise his voice again – but it doesn't come out so loud*): These people are preventing me from going in there . . .

KEVIN (*loud, agressive*): *No, we aren't . . . !*

CHARLOTTE: Nobody's listening to you at all. Look, nobody's watching – see!

KEVIN: They'll think you're drunk anyway.

NICK (*same tone*): These people are preventing me from leav . . .

KEVIN (*jumps*): Charlotte!

CHARLOTTE (*staring straight at him*): It's all right, he's going to pull himself together, isn't he . . . ?

NICK: These people are stopping me . . .

CHARLOTTE (*dangerous*): Nick, for the last time . . .

NICK (*gazing straight at her*): So you see I'm off now!

CHARLOTTE (*really savage*): JUST SHUT UP, NICK!

NICK *goes quiet.*

Silence.

CHARLOTTE: Thank you. That's better.

NICK (*quiet, clenched*): Right . . .

CHARLOTTE: You see that's better, isn't it – now.

KEVIN: And keep it like that.

NICK: Yes. (*He puts his hand into his pocket, pulls out a fistful of coins – then looks up at* CHARLOTTE.) I think I'm just going to make a phone call. (*Louder.*) I've got a lot of 2p's here. (*He holds out a fistful.*) Never had so many.

KEVIN (*by him still*): Christ, will you stop?

CHARLOTTE (*calmer*): Now, don't start it again, Nick.

NICK: No. I'm just going to make a quick call. Right! (*He looks straight at her.*) When *you've* gone, Charlotte.

Suddenly he moves abruptly, a step away from KEVIN – *and the coins drop all over the floor – spin everywhere.*
Silence.

NICK (*quiet – staring at them*): Oh Christ.

CHARLOTTE: What a mess. Why did you do that? Pick them up! I said pick them up!

NICK *doesn't move.* CHARLOTTE *picks up the coins.*

God the dust here, it's inches thick – and the smell.

KEVIN: There's one over here, I think. Can't see.

CHARLOTTE (*still by* NICK): Lot of muck here, all over the place. There's one here. (*She picks it up.*) We'll leave the rest, that's enough. We can't waste any more time. I'll be back in a moment. (*She goes.*)

KEVIN *moves across to the other side of the foyer, opposite* NICK, *who is by the 'safari' machine.*

KEVIN: Gone to change.

NICK (*hardly audible*): Yes.

KEVIN: Stay there, right.

He pulls the bottle of wine out of his pocket with an abrupt movement, then glances down at his clothes, then imme-diately looks up at NICK. *Muzak playing.*

I haven't got anything on me, have I?

NICK: What?

KEVIN (*glances down at his sleeve, then up at* NICK *again*): Haven't got anything on me? Don't think I have. . .

NICK: I don't know. (*He glances towards* KEVIN.) Yes, you have.

KEVIN, *keeping an eye on* NICK, *feels his clothes.*

No, you haven't.

KEVIN (*loud*): Got to see!

NICK (*suddenly loud*): For Christ sake!

KEVIN *stops feeling his clothes.*

You're all right.

KEVIN: Thanks. (*He thrusts the bottle forward.*) Have some of this.

NICK: No, thanks.

KEVIN (*loud*): HAVE SOME!

Silence.

Look, I know what's happened. It's . . . (Suddenly loud.) WELL, IT'S HAPPENED, SEE! (*He drinks, watching* NICK, *quieter, feeling the shock.*) It's happened . . .

NICK (*staring down at the floor*): Yes.

KEVIN: Charlotte won't be long. Don't worry, she won't be long. (*He is staring at* NICK, *and holding the bottle.*) It's hard for you, of course it is! (*Loud.*) We do realise that, you know. (*Gentle tone.*) But you're all right. You're with us. Just keep still. (*He drinks.*) This stuff works quickly, doesn't it – goes down you like razor blades. (*He thrusts it forward again.*) Have some!

NICK: No, thanks.

KEVIN (*opposite him, across the foyer*): You feel you're falling fast – (*He wipes his hair back.*) – head buzzing, want to lie down almost, you know, melt into it! You know, just lie down here, let the sounds drown it all out, put your head on the grass out there – you know, the green grass. (*Suddenly loud.*) Nick!

NICK (*looks up*): Yes . . .

KEVIN (*fast, jumpy*): Got to keep talking! Makes it better. Easier for you. (*Louder.*) It does!

NICK (*mechanically*): Easier?

KEVIN (*fast, straight at* NICK): I was at Glastonbury, you know. Yes! The Great Free Festival. (*Straight at him, loud, urgent:*) LISTEN TO THIS, NICK! One morning, it was Sunday morning. It was five o'clock. Dawn. Everybody asleep, and everything peaceful. There was this wonderful feeling in the air. It was so strong! You could almost touch it. There was a young singer on stage, just singing himself, nobody was listening. It was David Bowie – Yes! I was the only one up, almost; later, I was wandering about, in amongst all the people asleep, and I saw on the stage this *small white boy*, yes! All alone you know, about seven, standing with sun on his hair, smiling, really smiling you know, it was like the future, I just remembered it! That kid up there.

(*Savage at* NICK:) But things didn't go on like that, did they . . . ?

NICK: No. (*Not looking at* KEVIN.) Not for you, Kevin, no.

KEVIN (*really loud*): FOR NOBODY. FOR NOBODY AT ALL! (*Pause. To himself:*) Not so loud.

The noise of some vehicle arriving close by.

KEVIN (*glancing out, then at* NICK): What's that? Did you see? What is it?

NICK: A coach arriving . . .

KEVIN: Here! Arriving here.

NICK (*louder*): I don't know.

KEVIN: At the motel! Be at the motel. It's all right. (*Then urgent:*) We shouldn't be out here so long! (*He moves slightly, glances behind him for a split second.*) Charlotte'll be back in a moment. She knows what she's doing.

NICK (*mechanically*): Yes.

KEVIN: She does. It's going to be OK.

NICK (*quiet*): Yes, of course.

KEVIN (*loud*): It is you know!

NICK (*quiet, clenched*): Do you think he will count to ten – and then get up again, because it was only playing. (*Clenched, staring at the ground:*) Is that it?

KEVIN (back at him): People get killed on that road all the time. They do! Accidents. Probably one happening right at this moment. NOW. Often it's a type of murder, because there are too many cars out there, (*Straight at* NICK:) aren't there?

NICK (*quiet, clenched*): Of course. It makes sense now.

KEVIN (*loud, straight at him*): Well, aren't there?

NICK: Yes – Of course there are.

KEVIN (*straight at him*): You don't know how much is at stake, do you?

NICK: No, I don't.

KEVIN (*snaps*): Keep still, I told you. I suppose you think it's because of this trouble, my eye trouble, that I think

the things I do, feel what I do.

NICK (*quiet, clenched*): I don't know.

Pause. Muzak playing.

I don't know *what* you feel.

KEVIN: You can think what you like. But you're wrong, you know.

NICK: Yes, of course I am.

KEVIN (*serious*): Yes.

NICK (*clenched*): I'm not even sure how bad your eyes really are.

KEVIN: People always want superficial reasons for things. (*To* NICK:) They do, don't they. *So then they can dismiss them.* They want easy, obvious reasons for things. (*Loud, urgent:*) *Listen to this, Nick.* You really ought to, you know! But you see I've felt these things for a long time. Oh yes. Like a lot of people now. Know this place, this country *belongs to them.* Know it has to be protected.

NICK (*bewildered*): Protected . . .

KEVIN: It's not just a question of race – it's a question of England.

NICK (*clenched*): I'm not listening to this . . . (*Loud.*) I'm just not listening to this, Kevin, so you can . . . (*Very*

KEVIN (*very sharp*): Quiet, keep it quiet . . . (*He lowers his own voice, but it's really urgent, almost passionate.*) You've *got to listen, you see.* Maybe this trouble has made me realise things a little earlier, because it sharpens things, you know, thoughts, maybe I'm six months ahead, but only six months. I *know* a lot of people who feel this, people of my *age.* All of sorts. From young bankers to people like me. You don't believe me, of course, do you?

NICK: No.

KEVIN: But you *ought to.* I would show you the list, the list we're carrying, our contacts, but I'm not allowed to. Can't show that. That's why we *did* it. That's why it happened back there . . . we've got members all over the country. People full of disappointment . . . or whatever you call it.

NICK: Disappointment?

KEVIN: Or whatever you'd call it. (*Suddenly* KEVIN *whips round, looks over his shoulder.*) Where's Charlotte now? For Chrissake! Why is she being so long . . . ?

NICK (*quiet, clenched*): She had to clean herself up, didn't she?

KEVIN: Nothing can have happened, can it . . . ?

NICK: Of course not.

KEVIN: Then where is she? (*Intensely nervous, he calls out loud:*) Charlotte? (*He still keeps an eye on* NICK.) She didn't say she would be so long. (*Loud.*) Charlotte? (*He turns.*) She'll be back in a moment.

NICK: Yes.

KEVIN (*urgent*): We got to move from here! (*He stares straight at* NICK.) You know this now – this could be the beginning of a chase. (*Sharp.*) It probably is! A huge chase. We being hounded along the road. (*He looks at* NICK.) And if the police do catch up with us, *which they might do quite soon*, do you realise what that means?

NICK (*quiet, not looking at* KEVIN): Yes.

KEVIN (*staring straight at* NICK): Do you? I don't think you do. It means we stand a chance of becoming famous tonight, me and Charlotte, of becoming a sort of myth.

NICK (*clenched*): Kevin . . .

KEVIN: I know it sounds weird standing here, by this pathetic souvenir shop, in this dust, and this music, but you'll see on the radio, maybe soon; it might just be the beginning of a bit of a legend . . . something that will haunt people, young people. Following our route up here.

NICK (*louder, clenched*): Kevin – will you stop, just . . .

KEVIN: It may not happen – of course. *I really don't know.* (*Loud, sharp.*) We'll see, won't we! It could all be small and nasty. But *there is* a chance, if we get cornered and caught. (*Pause. Loud.*) Becoming a myth tonight! (*He stands staring at* NICK.) Yes! (*He

swings round. CHARLOTTE *is coming back in.*) Charlotte! She's back, it's all right.

CHARLOTTE *is wearing a clean new skirt and blouse. Pink or white, tight against her breasts. She is carrying the bag.*

CHARLOTTE: Right! Thank God that's done now.

NICK (*who is staring at her intently*): Yes! Feeling better are you?

CHARLOTTE: Yes I am. I've had a wash. (*Aggressive at* NICK.) I think you bruised my back just now – but I'm all right.

KEVIN (*concerned*): Do you want me to drive now Charlotte?

CHARLOTTE: No I'm fine. I can do it.

KEVIN: You must be very tired. I'll drive if you want, I will . . .

CHARLOTTE (*sharp*): No I'm fine. Come on now.

NICK (*suddenly moving from the machine*): You've put scent on haven't you, I can smell it.

CHARLOTTE (*determined to control him*): That's right.

NICK (*louder*): Put scent over it have you. All over it.

CHARLOTTE (*sharp*): Nick . . .

NICK (*up to her*): The dress is in the bag is it. (*Glancing down at it:*) Yes it is – stuffed in there.

KEVIN (*dangerous*): Leave her alone now for Chrissake. (*Warning:*) I told you . . .

NICK (*aggressive*): Why didn't you leave it in a basin. Just lying there.

CHARLOTTE (*firm*): Now don't start again will you . . .

NICK: Put scent all over – have you!

CHARLOTTE (*controlled*): Stop it Nick.

He is silent.

Right. (*She glances round, tenses slightly.*) We'll go out the way we came. Quickly. Walk straight to the van. We'll get as far as we can with the petrol we've got.

KEVIN: Yes, can't fill up here. (*Straight at* NICK:) Been here long enough.

CHARLOTTE (*staring at the exit*): Yes we have.

KEVIN *hands her handbag back.*
CHARLOTTE *takes it, tenses, straightens.*

(*Sharp.*) I'm ready then. (*She glances at the two men.*) Are both of you?

KEVIN: Yes.

CHARLOTTE *looks straight at* NICK – *pause.*

NICK: Yes.

CHARLOTTE: Good.

Blackout

Scene Two

*In the blackout we hear a disc-jockey on a late-night show chatting away . . . mentioning 'trouble on the road, bother in Doncaster, but for all of us that are safely tucked up, doing whatever you do when you're safely tucked up, on this hot night – yes, it is a bit hot for that, even for me! And that's saying a lot, here's . . .' He fades in a blast of music.
The lights come on an area outside the kitchens of another motorway cafe. Huge rubbish vats in the background; in the foreground a tarpaulin stretches over some crates, completely covering them.
Lights streaming from the kitchen doors.*
KEVIN, CHARLOTTE *and* NICK *by the tarpaulin.*
KEVIN *squatting by the radio moving the dials; blast of noise.*

CHARLOTTE: Not so loud . . .

KEVIN (*moving the dials*): It's all the late shows.

CHARLOTTE (*staring down at the radio*): Yes.

KEVIN: All the nights shows – yattering. Listen to them. (*He lets the disc-jockey pour out.*)

CHARLOTTE: Yes. Come on. (*She glances up.*) There's nobody in those

lorries over there? (*She stares.*) No.

NICK (*suddenly, staring down at the radio*): There isn't anything about it there! There isn't anything!

CHARLOTTE: Not so loud.

KEVIN (*moving the dials, exasperated – as commercials ring out*): It's just all of this pouring out.

Suddenly KEVIN *finds it. The fanfare for a news item.* * *They tense. Then the News comes out – the item announces a policeman has been found shot dead in Doncaster. It gives the exact location and 'two men and a woman were seen leaving the area'; they listen to it in silence.*

KEVIN (*as the first words of news item are read out*): There! (*Then he goes silent.*)

CHARLOTTE: Somebody saw us then. (*She moves away from the radio; the news has moved on to other things.*)

KEVIN *squats by the radio, he's holding a torch, he moves the dial.*

NICK: Yes! It seems they did.

KEVIN: They're out searching now . . .

CHARLOTTE: We must be eighty miles away.

KEVIN: A night search. Patrols, road blocks, spreading out in wider and wider circles. (*Quiet.*) I wonder if there's anymore. (*He flicks the dials some more.*)

CHARLOTTE: Not so loud!

KEVIN: Listen. There's some more. (*He hits the end of another news item about it. He moves the dial, and again we hear the end of a news item.*
KEVIN *is quiet, staring at the radio.*) It's everywhere, the whole machine is full of it. Totally crammed with it. (*He looks up at* NICK.) You see.

NICK (*quiet*): I see . . . A huge chase . . .

CHARLOTTE (*moves briskly*): I ought to phone Harrowby Street, but if the phones *are* tapped there . . . it's not worth the risk, is it?

———————————————
*For news items see page 53.

KEVIN: No, it isn't.

She is keeping a close watch on NICK. KEVIN *moves up to her, close, confidential.*

KEVIN: Are you cold now, Charlotte?

CHARLOTTE: Cold? No?

KEVIN: Good.

CHARLOTTE: Stay still, Nick.

KEVIN (*close, confidential, only half audible*): It's strange hearing it. You begin to feel it hasn't happened, a blank – but it has.

NICK (*loud, concerned*): What's he saying? What's he saying to you, Charlotte.

CHARLOTTE *moves.*

What was he saying to you?

CHARLOTTE: It's all right. Switch it off Kevin. Go on.

KEVIN *goes over to switch the radio off; as he squats by the radio, the* KID *enters.*

KEVIN: There! (*He switches it off.*)

KID: Hey . . .

They look up. The KID *is about seventeen, looks older, messy dazed appearance, nervy manner; he has obviously been through a lot of drugs.*

CHARLOTTE (*stiffens*): Yes – what is it?

KID: Have any of you got a light?

CHARLOTTE: I don't think we have. Has someone got a light for him?

Pause, nobody moves.

KID: I just want a light. (*Nobody moves.*) Come on! Somebody must have a light.

NICK (*suddenly*): Yes! Here.

KEVIN (*butting in*): No, I've got one. Here . . . (*He throws box of matches at* KID.)

KID: Ta.

CHARLOTTE: Right.

The KID *half moves, then turns.* CHARLOTTE *is leaning by the tar-*

paulin. Through this sequence KEVIN *moves close to* NICK.

KID: Can you – can you give me something for the juke-box, get some music, get the place back there going . . . wake it up.

CHARLOTTE: No. I'm afraid not . . .

KID: No, come on! The windows are open. You'll hear it too. Easily. So come on now. You can even choose the records if you like. Yuh . . . Have our own request programme . . .

CHARLOTTE: No.

KID (*moving towards her*): Can I join you then . . .

CHARLOTTE (*sharp*): No, you can't.

KID (*stopping*) You're wearing perfume, aren't you. Got perfume on.

NICK: Yes, she has . . .

KID: All over – I can smell it. (*To all of them.*) What you doing then?

CHARLOTTE (*very sharp and loud*): Nothing. We're just travelling!

KID (*turning to* KEVIN *and* NICK): You're going to give me something for the juke-box aren't you. Get some real dancing going . . .

KEVIN (*tense*): Look, we can't. OK . . .

KID: You're not meant to dance in these cafes. Indecent behaviour they call it. But I know a black chick that dances all night by herself in one of these places, should see the things she does. Christ! But she doesn't let anyone near her.

(*He suddenly looks at* CHARLOTTE.) She doesn't believe me.

KEVIN: She believes you. Right!

CHARLOTTE: Yes, you're talking about some black girl, could you just –

KID: Which way you going? Maybe I'm going that way myself. (*Broad grin.*) You never know – you might be lucky!

CHARLOTTE (*dipping into her bag*): There's the money, you can have it now . . .

KID: Ta! Great! (*He takes the money.*) Have I seen you round here before.

KEVIN (*very tense*): Why should you have . . . You couldn't have . . . so just . . .

NICK: Just take it. Go on.

KID (*straight on*): No reason. Sometimes I know people. I go hitching backwards and forwards along the road you see. I get to one end . . . do a few things then come straight back again.

KEVIN: Right. OK!

KID (*carrying straight on, moving around*): I know this road well now. And all the cafes! Been doing it for weeks. Some others do it too. It's catching on. But we don't tend to see each other much. You understand.

CHARLOTTE: Yes I do. Could you . . .

KID: It's great. Been in all sorts! Lorries, tankers, a Rolls-Royce. Christ! Yeah! . . . you get that sort on weekends, coming back from the country, where they go and stay.

KEVIN: Ok! – Look mate, we're in a hurry, so . . .

KID (*carrying straight on, ignoring him, fast*): I got a big Jaguar you see. And the back seat was completely covered in daffodils, and rhododendrons and things, thick with it, piled up, and right on top was a dead duck. Honest! Always look on the back seat. You see some really weird things.

CHARLOTTE: Could you leave us.

NICK: Just take it.

KID (*carrying on*): I got one car – this bloke kept looking at me all the time, then when I said I wanted to get out, he wouldn't stop the car you see. No! He said I looked like President Kennedy when he was young, the same expression; yeah, he had a huge hand. It came straight down on my trousers. Like a crane. Jaws! (*Suddenly.*) Are you listening? Are you listening to me?

CHARLOTTE: Yes. We are. But . . .

KID (*cutting her off*): What was I saying then?

Pause.

What was I saying? See – she doesn't know . . . I sleep in these places too,

you know. Have my own bench here, I call it my own. Crash out here.

KEVIN *is glancing at* CHARLOTTE.

CHARLOTTE: Listen – could you just leave us now.

KID: Christ, the dreams you get doing that! You have no idea. Really incredible dreams. Every quarter of an hour you get woken up. You can dream a hundred different things at night . . .

KEVIN (*really tense*): Look mate, we told you – we're in a hurry, so . . . just . . . (*Suddenly* KID *up to* CHARLOTTE, *by her*): Sometimes you know you're really dreaming of a nice body you know, like this one here, up against her, and she's doing things, Christ! The feeling! It *really is good*, really strong.

CHARLOTTE (*tense*): Is it?

KID: And you wake up at five o'clock in the morning, and you know the whole place by then is full of people, on every seat. Curled up! Wish I could wake up with her, that would be good, wouldn't it?

CHARLOTTE (*sharp, moving*): Look, I think we'll move on now, OK . . .

KID (*catching hold of her*): NO, you don't . . . NO. (*He grins.*) You want to see my tracks then. (*He begins to roll up his sleeve.*) You want to see them. You believed me! (*He shows arms.*) Actually, they don't show any more. Not much. (*Up by* CHARLOTTE.) Want to see them?

KEVIN (*suddenly loud*): Don't talk about that sort of thing. That muck! Right – just stop it!

KID (*grins, unabashed*): OK – she doesn't know what I'm talking about anyway.

CHARLOTTE (*really tense*): Unfortunately, I do.

KID (*up to her*): I saw an accident the other day, near here. I was really close. It was smashed all over the road. That was all right. She didn't like that, did she? (*Nervous grin.*) I don't blame her.

CHARLOTTE: Please would you leave us alone – could you just . . .

KID: It's great going up and down the road. You ought to do it. I might try London. It didn't work out for me before. I came down to London but it didn't work out.

CHARLOTTE (*clenched*): Please, just leave us alone, will you.

KID: Didn't get much to eat, you see . . .

CHARLOTTE (*really tense*): Look, you've got the money haven't you? *Would you go now?*

KID: I'm allowed to be here.

CHARLOTTE: But I'm asking you to leave. I find your being here – I don't find it very pleasant.

The KID is pressed up next to her on the tarpaulin.

KID: You can't stop me being here.

CHARLOTTE (*to* KEVIN): Are you going to get rid of him please?

KEVIN: Yeah – Come on, move. (KEVIN *is standing by* NICK.)

KID: I'm all right here, aren't I?

CHARLOTTE (*beginning to get desperate*): Are you going to go? (*She turns to the men.*) Come on, one of you, make him go away. (*Suddenly she screams.*) DON'T YOU UNDER-STAND, I CAN'T STAND HIM BEING NEAR ME – *DON'T YOU UNDERSTAND.*

KID: Listen, I'm only . . .

CHARLOTTE: You're filthy, you revolt me. (*She shouts.*) Go away, can't you. I can't stand him near me. I can't stand him near me.

KID: Are you nutty or something?

CHARLOTTE: MOVE HIM – (*Screaming.*) GO ON. GO. JUST GO AWAY. (*Screaming.*) JUST GET AWAY FROM ME. GET OUT.

The KID, stunned by her savagery moves away.

KID: Is she crazy or something – (*Loud.*) – is she?

CHARLOTTE (*very, very quiet*): I can't take this now.

KEVIN (*loud*): JUST GET AWAY FROM HERE. GET OUT.

KID (*aggressive*): I was just being here, wasn't I . . . I was just talking. Not allowed anymore, is it. Not allowed! (*He moves to the exit.*) Well, you've got it coming to you, – you fucking have.

Silence.

CHARLOTTE: He was filthy. I couldn't take it.

CHARLOTTE *starts to cry. Silence. Just her crying.*

KEVIN: Charlotte.

Pause. Just her crying.

NICK (*startled, only half hostile*): Charlotte . . .

CHARLOTTE: He was so disgusting. (*She cries. They watch. Suddenly, she clenches herself, pulls herself together.*) I'm sorry to make an exhibition of myself. I shouldn't have shouted. He was just so filthy. (*Her head flicks round.*) Don't move Nick.

KEVIN (*moving around, abrupt, nervous*): Do you – Charlotte – do you want anything?

CHARLOTTE: No. (*Suddenly it hits her they haven't done anything. Urgent:*) Come on. We've got to get on. Got to get the van filled up. Quickly, we can't stay here. They'll be coming down the road. (*Sharp to* KEVIN:) I said quickly.

KEVIN: Yes. I'll get her filled up now. (*He glances at* NICK.) I'll be back as quick as I can Charlotte. (*He goes.*)

CHARLOTTE *is lying on the tarpaulin facing* NICK.

CHARLOTTE (*sharp*): I'm all right now. Stay there.

Pause.

NICK (*fiddling nervously with the torch*): You realise! If a lorry comes out of the car park now, passes us now – he'd look down from his cab, and he'd see these people lying here, and he'll probably just think we're a couple of midnight picnickers or something – or even a couple of lovers lying by the kitchens, looking so normal. The pair of us. (*Aggressive.*) You're going to get seen any moment, you know.

CHARLOTTE: Are we!

Silence.

NICK (*staring at her*): You cried.

CHARLOTTE (*looking at him*): Yes, I did. That's right.

Music starts from the juke-box, continues through whole scene – the records changing.

CHARLOTTE: That kid . . . Listen to him.

NICK: Why are you lying down like that?

CHARLOTTE: Because you bruised my back when you pushed me, and it's hurting now.

NICK (*moves*): Is it?

CHARLOTTE (*really steely*): I told you not to move.

NICK: I know you did.

CHARLOTTE: Then don't. I've explained, haven't I, it's going to be all right if you do what we say. And if it suits us to be caught when the time comes, you could be a lot of use to us. So you really ought to believe me.

NICK (*quiet, but strong*): I'm not that stupid Charlotte.

CHARLOTTE: It's your own choice anyway. We don't want you to get hurt. Do you think we want to hurt. Just for the fun, seeing . . .

NICK (*sharp*): I wouldn't know about that, would I?

CHARLOTTE (*steely*): You think we enjoyed what happened back there, do you . . . Is that what you think, you bastard? That's what you believe, is it?

NICK (*watching her*): I don't know.

CHARLOTTE (*steely*): Is it?

NICK: No.

CHARLOTTE (*quieter*): That's better. Then keep still, will you. (*Watching him:*) Have you broken that torch?

NICK: What?

CHARLOTTE: Have you broken it?

NICK: What does it matter? It doesn't work now.

CHARLOTTE: Then would you mend it.

NICK (*quiet*): Mend it!

CHARLOTTE: We may need it.

NICK (*pulls it to pieces*): My hand's shaking.

CHARLOTTE: I keep expecting to hear a siren any moment . . . I hope Kevin's going to be all right.

NICK (*loud*): Why shouldn't he be all right?

CHARLOTTE (*anxious*): I wonder how long he'll be . . . I hardly knew him before today, strange isn't it . . . I hope he hurries!

NICK (*loud*): Why are you talking about Kevin all the time for Chrissake. I'm here, and you're going to talk to me now, yes, whether you want to or not.

She looks at him.

Right. (*He looks down.*) I don't know what I'm doing with this torch. It's in pieces, the spring's gone.

CHARLOTTE: Give it here then – come on, give it to me.

NICK *lifts the torch.*

Just hand it to me.

NICK *leans forward and hands it to her, and in doing so, moves closer.*

NICK: My hands are so sticky, I couldn't grip it.

CHARLOTTE fiddles with torch; we see her nerves.

CHARLOTTE: There. (*She flicks the torch, it works; she shines it in his face.*) I've done it.

NICK (*aggressive*): You're nervous now, aren't you – aren't you?

CHARLOTTE: Of course.

NICK (*charged*): Have you got brothers and sisters?

Pause.

Come on, have you got brothers and sisters?

CHARLOTTE: Brothers and sisters!

NICK: Don't just repeat it.

CHARLOTTE: A young brother.

Music playing.

NICK (*sharp*): And your parents?

CHARLOTTE: Yes?

NICK: Are you close to your parents?

CHARLOTTE: Close?

NICK (*very loud*): DON'T just repeat it.

CHARLOTTE: Quite close really.

NICK: Yes. Go on. You're going to talk. Go on . . .

CHARLOTTE: How long will he be do you think?

NICK: Forget about Kevin. Go on . . . Charlotte. (*He moves nearer.*)

CHARLOTTE: Don't move. I told you. I don't want you any closer. (CHARLOTTE *moves herself up on the taupaulin.*) You *really* did hurt my back. It's shooting through me now. (*Real determination.*) But I'm going to make it go. I can! (*She is lying propped up – staring down at* NICK.) When I was small, I once went swimming in a lake near us in the country. In Kent, quite a lovely part really.

NICK: Yes. Go on . . . Go on!

CHARLOTTE: It's not like that any more of course. Completely ruined. The middle of the fruit country. The water was very thick with mud and oil and things, filthy and very hot . . . How far are we from the road? (*She stops.*)

NICK: Go on.

CHARLOTTE: And I thought if I could bring myself to swim underwater in thi filth I can do anything. I can do just about anything. And I did do it! You see. I went under – yes. I couldn't see anything except a sort of horrid muzzy darkness. It went all over me and in me. Over my mouth like a mud gag. (*Suddenly.*) It feels like that now doesn't it, all the time. (*Watching him.*) Doesn't it? Put your hand over your mouth and hold it there – go on, put your hand over your mouth.

NICK (*half raises his hand*): No –

CHARLOTTE: That's what it felt like – feels like – all the time, for a lot of people.

Pause.

NICK: Go on . . . Go on.

CHARLOTTE: I got out and walked for miles down the path through *our* fields, I was working things out, I was only fourteen. I wouldn't do that now. I was a ridiculous child in many ways. But I thought a lot – when I was on my own. (*She shifts slightly and winces in pain.*)

Music playing. Pause.

NICK (*sharp, staring at her*): Go on! The things going on in your head, Charlotte . . .

CHARLOTTE: You don't know anything about that. (*Straight at him.*) You don't know what's going on at all.

NICK (*leaning towards her, forceful, not hysterical*): Oh yes – the girl from the county estate, a beautiful house, who had everything she wanted, always, right, didn't she?

CHARLOTTE (*loud*): Don't move.

NICK (*carrying straight on*): No! Worried about what's happening to England, worried that things might get worse for her, so blame it on the Blacks, so round them up, ship them off, of course, ship them away, out to sea – (*Shouting:*) – and then, of course, anything else that's offensive, remove that as well.

CHARLOTTE(*loud*): STOP IT, NICK –

I mean it.

Pause. He is nearer her.

You won't ever shout at me again.

NICK (*defiant*): NO!

Pause.

Go on – Go on, Charlotte – (*He stares straight at her.*) Tell me *everything* now – tell me about the English People's Party –

CHARLOTTE: I've told you all you're going to know. (*She glances round.*) Why is he being so long? Where is he?

NICK (*forceful*): Forget him! (*He leans towards her on the tarpaulin.*) Why were you carrying a gun, Charlotte? Come on, tell me –

CHARLOTTE: To protect myself.

NICK: Protect yourself against what?

CHARLOTTE: Against all the leftist groups that know what we're doing.

NICK: What leftist groups?

CHARLOTTE (*steely*): All of them. They're armed too. They've been acquiring arms all the time . . .

NICK: You really believe that.

CHARLOTTE (*fierce*): It's not a question *of believing* . . .

NICK (*louder, closer*): You really believe there are hundreds of armed people moving all over the country *tonight* . . .

CHARLOTTE: Yes. It's increasing all the time. Don't come any closer, Nick . . . I mean it.

Pause. Music playing.

A lot of people may experience it soon.

NICK: Experience what?

CHARLOTTE: Where is he? He should be back.

NICK (*loud*): Experience what –

Pause.

CHARLOTTE: Having to kill someone. Seeing them fall. (*She looks straight at him. Loud:*) You have no idea what's happening – none at all, have you?

You believe nothing's really going on at all – don't you? (*Sudden, straight at him.*) There's a civil war coming . . . in eighteen months, in two years. I don't want it to happen, but we can see it coming . . .

NICK (*forceful*): So that's what you're trying to do is it? Whipping people up. Making people believe all this . . .

CHARLOTTE: There'll be guerilla-style clashes to begin with.

NICK (*strong*): But you won't manage it, Charlotte, unless you're allowed to.

CHARLOTTE (*suddenly letting it pour out*): And they'll escalate – and keep on escalating. It's already nearly happening. The Left disrupting meetings, like they disrupt everything, preventing freedom of speech all the time. Running down England, bringing this country to its knees, killing it, you just have to read their press, to see what they're intending to do.

NICK (*quiet, forceful*): Charlotte, you don't really –

CHARLOTTE (*straight back*): YES, I do.

Pause.

(*She's now worked up.*) When did you last feel happy about the future? (*Loud:*) When? Tell me.

NICK: Often. (*Loud.*) I often –

CHARLOTTE (*straight back*): When? When did you? Five years ago? Ten years ago? When you left school? all those wasted years of grey government, letting the country be overrun – people who just don't belong.

NICK (*clenched*): You don't know what you're saying, Charlotte . . .

CHARLOTTE: Where has it got anybody, anybody at all, everything sliding, sliding so fast! And they're powerless to stop it. Everything been grey for so long, and the mess, everywhere, just totally grey. (*She looks at him, quieter.*) Like you . . .

NICK (*defiant*): Like me? –

Silence. They face each other.

CHARLOTTE (*with controlled passion*): Look at this – look at it, here. (*She gazes out across the landscape.*) This sprawling mess, those lights up there, that savage light, have you ever seen something so horrible, anything so inhuman, more disgusting, it's just degrading. It presses down on us all. (*Loud.*) Do you know what used to be here – where we are now. DO YOU? A valley and fields. It did. How can people live with a dread of the future all the time. How can you bring people up like that – just offer them that all the time. Tell me. Somebody's got to do something.

Silence. With an abrupt movement, NICK gets onto the bottom of the tarpaulin, much nearer CHARLOTTE. She flinches away – a few feet between them.

CHARLOTTE (*fierce*): DON'T!

Pause. He lies there.

(*Steely calm.*) You shouldn't have done that, Nick.

NICK: No. (*Pause. Near her.*) No I know I shouldn't. (*Quiet.*) Do you think about him at all.

CHARLOTTE: Who?

NICK (*louder*): And maybe his family – are you thinking about it . . .

CHARLOTTE (*steely*): Didn't I tell you not to raise your voice. And you've moved even closer – haven't you –

Pause.

Don't try to touch me.

NICK: No.

The music finishes.

CHARLOTTE (*her head flicks slightly*): The music's stopped. (*Pause – suddenly loud.*) Where is he? Where's Kevin? (*Really urgent.*) WHERE'S KEVIN – ?

NICK: He's not come back –

CHARLOTTE: No.

NICK stretches out his hand slightly, but only tentatively.

(*Calm.*) Don't do that . . .

NICK (*quiet*): Your cardigan's soaked . . . look at it, it's completely soaked in sweat.

CHARLOTTE: It's because it's hot, isn't it? It's an old cardigan.

NICK (*quiet*): An old one . . . it's probably one of your mother's – isn't it. You could wring it out – it's so wet.

CHARLOTTE: I told you not to try to touch me.

NICK (*quiet, straight at her*): You really must be in pain, mustn't you?

CHARLOTTE: Don't tell me what I'm feeling.

NICK: Yes – your eyes are watering. I can see it.

CHARLOTTE: And if I am. Whose fault is that?

NICK (*quiet*): That's right . . . yes. And you're lying on some oil, it's all over you.

CHARLOTTE: I'm all right. It's only a bruise after all.

She suddenly sits up bolt upright on the tarpaulin, flinches with the pain, then straightens. NICK moves back instinctively.

There. (*She straightens her back with effort.*) It's gone. See – it's gone.

NICK: Yes. The oil's all over your back, Charlotte . . .

CHARLOTTE (*staring straight at him*): I know.

NICK: You realise, Charlotte, we're about the same age, you and me.

CHARLOTTE: Yes.

NICK (*suddenly loud*): What are you really expecting to happen – tonight – (*Pause.*) What you're expecting?

CHARLOTTE: I don't know. We were *seen*, that's all we know. (*She looks at him across the tarpaulin.*) Are you going to move of your own accord Nick?

They face each other.

NICK: No. You're very thin, aren't you, Charlotte?

CHARLOTTE: Yes.

NICK (*staring at her*): I don't see – I just don't . . . You're not even a very intelligent girl, are you? You aren't. Not deep inside there. Not even very bright. You've no ideas at all, nothing, except shabby, vicious, second-hand thoughts. (*Forceful.*) Why am I still here, Charlotte – I could have easily . . .

CHARLOTTE: No. You couldn't.

NICK (*forceful*): I really don't know why I didn't . . .

CHARLOTTE (*quiet, staring at him*): Because until now you were being sensible, weren't you . . . and it was all right.

NICK (*quiet, firm*): Was I? I'm not moving from here Charlotte. I warn you – I'm not moving.

KEVIN *enters.*

CHARLOTTE: He's here.

KEVIN *stands staring at him.*

KEVIN: Go on – leave her.

NICK *doesn't move.*

I said LEAVE HER.

NICK: NO!

Pause. Silence.

I'm not moving, Kevin.

A moment's pause, as NICK *lies by* CHARLOTTE *on the tarpaulin –* CHARLOTTE *then, with a sudden movement, gets up, moves off the tarpaulin.*

KEVIN: Yes! Are you all right, Charlotte . . .

CHARLOTTE (*sharp*): I'm fine now. Absolutely fine.

KEVIN (*loud*): I've done it. And paid! I thought I was going to be short – I thought I didn't have enough, I thought I'd have to come back. But I did have enough!

CHARLOTTE: Right.

KEVIN (*loud*): We've got enough to go the whole way . . .

The KID *enters.*

CHARLOTTE: Oh God . . .

KID: Hello –

KEVIN (*dangerous*): What you want?

KID: I was wondering since you're still here, and just filled you van up – how about a lift –

KEVIN (*tense*): A lift –

KID: Yeah – I've been here eight hours.

CHARLOTTE (*steely*): Have you . . . ?

NICK (*nervous*): Christ . . .

KID: And can't get a lift. I want to be moving, can't stay here any longer. I've been here eight hours! Got to get away. Come on – give me a lift –

CHARLOTTE: NO.

NICK: Just leave, go on – I'm telling you – leave –

KID: Just to the next cafe – come on – you're going to give me a lift.

CHARLOTTE: Get rid of him –

KEVIN: We told you once.

KID: I want a lift. It won't hurt you.

NICK: Just get out will you –

KID: No. I'm going to get a lift.

KEVIN (*dangerous*): Are you going to go?

KID: No.

KEVIN *throws himself at the kid, shouting 'Just get out'. The* KID *fights back really viciously –* NICK *suddenly follows* KEVIN, *catching hold of the* KID's *head, shouting 'Just leave'. The* KID *breaks away from* KEVIN, *and* NICK *catches hold of him. A siren is heard faintly in the distance.*

CHARLOTTE: For Chrissake – (*As the fight goes on:*) Just get rid of him – that's all.

The KID *fights viciously with* NICK; KEVIN *goes for him too;* NICK *drags the* KID *away.*

NICK: Just go. Right. (*He lets the* KID *go.*)

KID (*stunned*): I don't . . . (*Very quiet, dazed.*) What's the matter with you? (*He goes.*)

NICK *stares at* CHARLOTTE, *then at* KEVIN. CHARLOTTE *looks at both of them.*

CHARLOTTE (*quiet*): Thank you.

The siren suddenly starts again, approaching fast.

They stand, still, as it approaches.

The siren increases, really loud, getting incredibly close – then it roars past.

CHARLOTTE (*as soon it passes while it's still dying*): Gone past.

KEVIN (*big grin of relief*): Yes!

CHARLOTTE: Come on – pick the things up. We've got to be moving.

Blackout

Scene Three

The hillside. Dark. Blankets and thermos spread out. KEVIN, CHARLOTTE, NICK, *leaning up against a low stone wall or a grassy bank.*
In the blackout a strong radio bulletin* is heard about the night search, which cuts into the radio on stage. At end of bulletin CHARLOTTE *gets up, moves across abruptly to the radio and switches it off.*

CHARLOTTE (*sharp*): Right! (*She crosses over and sits down, she has some crumpled writing paper with her, and a biro, puts them on her lap.*)

Silence. They all stare out.

KEVIN (*matter of fact*): Christ it's quiet. (*Pause.*) Terrifyingly quiet suddenly. (*Loud to* NICK:) Isn't it?

NICK: Yes.

NICK *is nervously tying the lace on his desert boots.*

KEVIN (*feeling the bank with the palm of his hand*): And the ground's so hard, baked hard. (*Loud.*) This heat –

it really does feel as if it's before *something enormous.*

CHARLOTTE (*scribbling on the paper*): Yes.

KEVIN (*staring out*): You can just see the edge of the road – curling round. (*Loud.*) See it! Cutting through!

CHARLOTTE: Yes. Not so loud.

KEVIN (*mechanically*): Not so loud.

CHARLOTTE: And keep your heads down both of you.

KEVIN: Yes. (*Pause.*) What you writing all the time, Charlotte?

CHARLOTTE: It's all right . . . (*Very tense.*) I've nearly finished. I can't concentrate now, though, the pen keeps slipping – all the time. (*She suddenly looks up at* NICK; *unnaturally loud:*) Stop that! The lace is broken Nick.

NICK: Yes, I know. I know it is.

KEVIN: Going to stand up.

CHARLOTTE: Why?

KEVIN: I want to . . . They can't see . . . (*But he keeps upstage. Staring out.*) Do you think they're out there now, slipping silently into place? Cars driving across the fields . . .

CHARLOTTE (*quiet*): I don't know . . .

KEVIN: Moving through the long grass – encircling the whole hillside. They could well be doing that. (*Suddenly loud.*) Yes – there's a light, I think. See –

CHARLOTTE: Where? Where is it?

KEVIN: You see it? I think . . . no, it's gone. (*Pause.*) I can't see, can you?

CHARLOTTE: It's gone.

Siren sounds in the distance.
CHARLOTTE *glances round, tense.*

There they are anyway.

KEVIN: Yes. (*Glancing behind them.*) Out there somewhere.

CHARLOTTE: It's quite a way off still.

KEVIN: Yes, it is.

Siren playing around in the distance.

*For news items see page 53.

Getting nearer though.

CHARLOTTE: Slowly, yes.

The siren dies.

NICK (*sharp but quiet*): Looking forward to it, are you . . . ?

CHARLOTTE: I don't know. (*She glances down at the paper, matter-of-fact.*) I don't know what I feel . . .

NICK (*louder*): Looking forward to it, are you . . . ?

CHARLOTTE (*stares straight at him*): Just don't begin that again.

KEVIN (*quiet, moving downstage slightly*): You realise we would just have to fire first. We just have to fire the first shot – to unleash a whole stream from out there. A complete onslaught.

NICK (*sharp*): Kevin.

KEVIN: They shoot to kill . . . they do in fact.

NICK: Kevin, don't you . . .

KEVIN (*quiet, cutting him off*): It's the truth. Haven't you read the papers . . . They shoot to kill . . . (*Pause.*) Whole burst from there. They'll smash straight into us.

NICK (*quiet, aggressive*): Smash into you?

Silence.

CHARLOTTE (*with the thermos, quiet*): Have some. (*She holds it out to KEVIN.*) Come on, I don't want any but you have some.

KEVIN *takes the thermos, takes a short drink.*

NICK (*suddenly loud*): Christ . . . What do you want now, Charlotte?

CHARLOTTE: I don't know. (*She takes the thermos from KEVIN.*) It's all right . . . (*Then to NICK, as she holds out the thermos.*) Have some?

NICK: No.

CHARLOTTE *puts the thermos down beside her.*

What you hoping for then? (*Pause.*) Charlotte Pearson and Kevin Gellot

. . . (*Pause, nervous but controlling it.*) See that – written on the streets?

KEVIN (*staring out*): Yes . . .

NICK: Is that what you want . . . ? Staring out of all the hoardings, Charlotte and Kevin . . . up there, huge . . . blow by blow account , . . all this . . . blow by blow . . .

CHARLOTTE(*calm*): Quieter . . .

NICK: In the papers . . . in the supplements too, pages about you.

KEVIN: Yes.

NICK (*loud*): What do you mean, Yes? (*Louder.*) What do you mean . . .

CHARLOTTE: Don't move around . . . I told you . . .

Pause.

NICK (*looking down, pulling at the grass, short abrupt movements*): Yes . . . up on people's walls, above their beds, life-size . . . is that what you want . . . The martyrs . . . for those school kids whose minds you hope to poison. Hope to *infect*.

CHARLOTTE: Just try to keep still.

Siren – same distance as before.

There it is . . . same distance, isn't it . . . circling still . . .

KEVIN: Yes. It is.

Pause, as the siren plays around.

Bound to find us sooner or later, England's such a small country . . .

The siren dies.

NICK: You've knocked the thermos over – it's spilling. (*Sharp.*) Pick it up . . .

CHARLOTTE: Yes. (*She does so.*)

Pause.

NICK (*pulling at the grass, looking down*): You can see that, can't you . . . the faces in the dock. Staring out. Both of you. Pale faces. Your hair cut short. And the headlines . . . all that muck . . . the hundreds of headlines. Charlotte Pearson – the girl . . . and Kevin Gellot – the half-blind companion . . . (*Pause – still looking down.*) Yes, you can see the pictures. Just for a moment you can see them. Clearly . . . (*Loud.*) But it's not going to happen like you want. (*Loud.*) It isn't you know . . . (*Pause. Pulling at the grass, to himself.*) It hasn't happened yet . . .

KEVIN (*staring out*): Maybe not . . .

NICK: Because you're alone.

CHARLOTTE (*moving her position slightly, against bank*): I haven't slept for 24 hours, you know. I've never been without sleep for so long. It's an extraordinary feeling. (*She brushes her hair back with her hand.*)

KEVIN: No, nor have I. (*He goes over to* CHARLOTTE, *quiet, close, confidential.*) I hardly slept at all the night before. Before this one. Because I was thinking about this trip – this journey of ours. I couldn't have slept for more than an hour. (*He is right beside her.*) Not more than an hour, Charlotte.

CHARLOTTE: No.

KEVIN: How's your back?

NICK: What you saying to her?

CHARLOTTE: It's better now. It's fine.

NICK (*loud*): What you saying to each other?

CHARLOTTE: It's all right, Nick. Stay there. (*Tense.*) We'll know very soon. It gets light very quick, see . . . it comes up so swiftly at this time of year. Just have to prepare ourselves.

KEVIN (*by her, quiet, matter-of-fact*): Yes, I know.

CHARLOTTE (*looking at* KEVIN, *gently but matter-of-fact*): Quiet . . . that's right, that's better.

KEVIN: Not much time now . . .

CHARLOTTE: No. I've written it down. Everything . . . What we stand for. I couldn't finish it . . . I've just scrawled it down . . . I don't want to show it, it's not how I'd like to have put it. But it's almost all there – everything.

NICK (*louder*): Charlotte?

CHARLOTTE: Just stay there.

NICK (*loud, aggressive*): Tell me as we then . . .

CHARLOTTE: I am telling you . . . (*She glances down at the paper.*) So it down there now.

KEVIN *suddenly gets up, moves dow stage.*

Where you going?

KEVIN: Show myself.

CHARLOTTE: Why?

KEVIN *stands downstage.*

KEVIN (*loud*): It's all right! Nothing so far! We're in a good position for it, aren't we? In a really good position – the best we could have. (*Suddenly.*) You know what happened here? You know what happened on this hillside, that valley? It's a battlefield – an old battlefield. No, it's true. I know abou it. The Wars of the Roses, right here, by these gorse bushes, in these fields. Under the ground, under this earth, there're pieces of England, lying right under the surface, under this grass. Scrape it away, scrape away the top, and you'll find it, it'll be staring up at you, out of the ground! The whole history of the place. (*Suddenly really loud.*) AND YOU CAN'T CHANGE THAT!

CHARLOTTE (*quiet, firm*): NO.

KEVIN: There should be a monument here. 150 feet high. Thick, granite! Unmoveable, yes, up on top of this hill. I know all about it, because we came up here, years ago now, it seems, that's why I knew we had to stop here. Because I saw it! I recognised it! (*He smiles.*) There was lot of us that came up, a whole lot of us round here then, in Northumberland. It was like our own village, all o us together, here, building things, making things, living under this sky. Peacefully. It was incredible. Spread over here. 50 of us – you should have seen it, the colour and the feeling then! And it lasted all that year. (*Loud.*) I passed through that wood just now, coming up. I saw the remain of it all, the bits of it lying there. The bits we built, rotting and covered in wire, and sawn into pieces, broken up! Old nails sticking out – you could tear yourself on it now, rip your leg open, get diseased. You could. And the pool where we used to swim. Dried up, of course, rusted up, and filled in, full of filth, where we used to be all the time . . . (*Loud, fast, suddenly letting rip.*) WHAT'S HAPPENED TO THEM? Tell me that. What's happened to them all?

ICK (*tensing*): Kevin . . .

EVIN (*carrying straight on*): I see a face in the street sometimes. I hardly recognise it, it's changed so much. Exhausted, eaten into. Without a job, of course, they always are, or just about to lose one, limping along, unable to do anything, almost broken, no life for anything. Shadows. (*Loud.*) Just shadows, of course. But that is changing now. It is.

HARLOTTE: Yes. It is.

ICK (*tensing*): Charlotte . . .

EVIN (*carrying straight on*): People have had enough now – they have! This summer is different. Under the heat, it's all changing.

HARLOTTE: Yes . . .

The light is increasing, getting brighter all the time.

EVIN: A kind of turning point, yes! This is going to be quite a famous summer, it really is. It's the end of an era – end of this appalling era, isn't it, yes. (*Really loud.*) And if we're the first, the first of our age, to become really known, show what's happening, *then we're the first!* And there it is!

HARLOTTE: Yes.

ICK (*loud*): Charlotte . . .

EVIN (*loud*): Just look at this! This is one of the most beautiful parts of England. This here! See it now. It's totally unspoiled – untouched. It's ours still. You just have to open your mouth here, and it'll roll over five counties, it will. There's nothing in the way. *They haven't ruined it yet.*

HARLOTTE (*sharp*): and it's going to stay that way.

KEVIN: Yes. It is. It's not full of people that don't belong.

NICK (*dangerous*): Stop it, Kevin – are you going to stop?

KEVIN: That just shouldn't be here! That never ought to have been allowed to come – they've got to be sent back now! Back to where they came from. Yes! Even the kids in school are beginning to feel it, feel their Englishness know this place belongs to them . . .

NICK (*jumps up, grabs* KEVIN): Kevin, just stop it! Do you hear? STOP IT!

CHARLOTTE (*shouts*): Let him go . . .

KEVIN: Get off me . . .

NICK (*shaking him really hard*): Just stop that, once and for all. Stop it.

KEVIN: Let go of me . . . (*Pause.*) Go on – let go.

Silence. NICK *lets go of his arm.*

CHARLOTTE: That's right.

NICK (*staring at* KEVIN): Kevin . . . Racing with it, aren't you . . . (*He glances at* CHARLOTTE.) Look at him . . . still racing through him . . .

Pause.

KEVIN (*quiet*): You don't feel anything, do you? You have no idea what to do at all.

The siren starts again, much nearer.

CHARLOTTE: Sit down, both of you. (*Dangerous:*) Sit down –

KEVIN: It's much nearer.

The siren is approaching, but is not on top of them yet.

Isn't it? They're going to get to us now.

CHARLOTTE (*really tense*): Maybe. Move back. Against this.

They move against the bank, tense.

Right back.

NICK (*loud, strong*): Charlotte?

KEVIN (*nervous*): It's gone quiet again. (*He glances behind him.*) Where are they now?

NICK (*his voice strong, bold*): Charlotte

– look at me a moment.

The lights are coming up to full brightness during the exchange between NICK *and* CHARLOTTE.

(NICK *is suddenly really authoritative.*) Charlotte?

CHARLOTTE (*really sharp*): Don't move . . . Just sit there . . .

NICK (*loud, angry, very strong*): Look at me, Charlotte.

CHARLOTTE *turns her head, and looks at him.*

That's better. You look different this morning.

CHARLOTTE: Do I?

NICK: Yes you do . . . messy.

She turns.

No! Look at me now. (*Quietly powerful.*) So you believe all this obscene muck, do you . . . ?

CHARLOTTE (*not understanding*): What?

NICK: You heard me. All this obscene muck.

She looks down.

(*Very strong.*) No, keep looking, keep looking at me. (*Really loud.*) Look at me, Charlotte . . .

CHARLOTTE (*turns her head*): Yes?

NICK: You believe all that, do you – ALL OF IT?

CHARLOTTE (*quiet*): You've been told.

NICK: I mean, Kevin's finished now, completely finished.

KEVIN (*dangerous*): That's right.

NICK (*strong, staring at her*): But you – with you, there's a crack, isn't there, just a crack, but it's there, (*Really loud.*) isn't there?

CHARLOTTE (*quiet, tone distant*): I don't know what you're talking about.

NICK: Just a slight one – but it's there, after this night. Yes! (*Strong.*) Because you don't believe quite all of it, do you? Not deep down. Not the *whole lot.* You can't believe quite all of it can

you Charlotte.

CHARLOTTE: I don't understand what he's saying. (*She glances towards* KEVIN.)

NICK: Don't look at him – he won't help – look at me, Charlotte!

KEVIN: What's he saying – what's he talking about?

CHARLOTTE (*distant, uncomprehending*): I don't know what he's saying.

NICK (*loud*): Yes you do – you can't quite believe *everything*, can you. And you know you're completely alone, too. (*Forceful.*) Come on, Charlotte. You know what I mean – you know exactly what I'm saying. (*Strong.*) Come on –

CHARLOTTE: I've told you everything (*Quiet.*) It's not worth the effort to try any more.

NICK: Come on – that's not good enough, is it, Charlotte? That just won't do – will it? (*Urgent.*) Come on

CHARLOTTE: If he doesn't understand now – he never will –

NICK: Won't he? BUT I DO UNDERSTAND.

CHARLOTTE (*staring right back*): Do you?

KEVIN (*staring out*): I'm not sure if there's anyone out there . . .

NICK (*loud, passionate*): And I'm going to get it out of you, Charlotte. I AM –

KEVIN: What's he saying to you?

CHARLOTTE (*very distant*): I don't know. I really don't know.

KEVIN: Just leave her.

NICK (*watching her*): NO. Not now –

CHARLOTTE: I've told you everything.

NICK (*really loud*): I told you – that won't do, Charlotte – *I know.* I know, deep down, inside there, right in there you don't believe it all, and I'm going to prise it out of you, Charlotte. You're going to say it, you are.

Pause.

(*Urgent.*) Now, come on. Tell me. Tell me.

CHARLOTTE (*very distant, calm*): Will you stop this now. I don't understand at all.

NICK (*suddenly catching hold of her arm*): *I mean for Chrissake* you're almost a normal girl, aren't you, I mean in other circumstances people wouldn't look twice, normal little rich girl, I mean, lots more like you – (*By her face.*) There's nothing special there at all. Is there. NOTHING.

Pause.

(*Strong.*) So come on now – tell me, Charlotte –

CHARLOTTE: Just leave me alone. I don't understand.

KEVIN: Leave her.

NICK: I'm talking to you, Charlotte, aren't I? Come on, tell me. (*Suddenly really shouting, emotional, tightening his grip on her arm.*) You're wrong. And you know you're wrong. You do. And you're going to say it. You are! Even if I have to break that head open . . . *Come* on *Charlotte* . . . *Come* on! (*Slightly quieter:*) You really know you are . . . You do.

Pause.

(*Much quieter.*) Come on.

CHARLOTTE (*quieter, matter-of-fact*): You've still no idea at all, have you?

NICK (*quieter, but still quite forceful*): Haven't I?

CHARLOTTE (*quiet*): No idea at all.

NICK (*quieter*): *I* see . . .

Pause.

(*Quiet, matter-of-fact.*) Come on . . . tell me.

The lights are now up to full.

KEVIN (*suddenly loud*): There isn't anyone out there! Look, there isn't!

CHARLOTTE (*looks out*): No, there isn't.

KEVIN (*loud*): They've gone past –

CHARLOTTE (*slight smile*): I thought they might.

KEVIN (*loud*): They've gone by again! Right by! (*He smiles.*) We're alone up here.

CHARLOTTE: Yes. Just the tractor down there. God, my clothes feel rough . . .

KEVIN (*staring out*): Three hundred feet down to there. Look. A dewy morning. There's no wind at all, is there – completely still –

CHARLOTTE: Come on – we must leave at once. Right now – they'll be back very soon. Pick everything up, Kevin – (*She snaps:*) Quick.

KEVIN *moves with speed.*

We're moving on now, Nick – (*To KEVIN:*) Come on, quickly, that blanket as well – (CHARLOTTE *folds the blanket.*) – take them to the van.

KEVIN: That's everything – (*He takes his dark glasses off.*)

CHARLOTTE: Yes, Kevin –

KEVIN: Goodbye then, mate.

NICK: Goodbye.

KEVIN *hesitates for a split second.*

CHARLOTTE: Go on, Kevin, quickly. I'll bring these.

KEVIN *goes;* CHARLOTTE *finishes folding the blanket.*

NICK: You're going now?

CHARLOTTE: Yes.

NICK (*quiet*): Good.

CHARLOTTE: Yes. (*Matter-of-fact.*) Finish the trip. (*She puts the blanket on top of the big bag, and picks up the thermos.*)

NICK (*staring out, not at CHARLOTTE*): I see. (*Quiet.*) If someone was standing right over there, we'd just be two small dots on a hillside, you realise. (*Quiet, he moves his head slightly.*) God, it's still, isn't it? Suddenly there's no wind at all. He's right. Just quiet.

CHARLOTTE: Yes. Don't turn round

now, Nick.

NICK: What?

He turns, she's holding the gun. Split
second between them.

Charlotte?

She shoots him – very close range.
She picks up the bag and the thermos
and leaves.
On the soundtrack we hear the sound
of traffic news on the wireless getting
louder and louder, brash, jarring names
of by-passes and road intersections
blasting out fiercely. Then total silence.

Fade.

End of play

FIRST NEWSCAST
(Scene Six)

Fanfare for news.

ANNOUNCER: Independent Radio
News, at one o'clock. This is David
Williams.
A police constable was shot dead in
Doncaster tonight. His body was found
in the North West of the city at about
10.30. Police are not revealing his
identity until relatives have been
informed. Here is Ken Lewis in
Doncaster.

KEN LEWIS: At around ten o'clock
tonight a young police constable, out
on his normal beat was shot dead at
point blank range here in Clive Road,
in the North West of Doncaster. He
was found out on the pavement here,
by the side of the old Granada
Cinema. He had been shot four times.
This is a fairly deserted area of the
city, the cinema like most of the
surrounding area is awaiting demoli-
tion, and the police are urgently
requesting anybody that may have seen
some people leaving the area hurriedly
at about ten tonight to come forward.
They already believe that more than
one person was involved, and are
interviewing witnesses who heard the
sound of the shots.
Road blocks have been set up all
around the city and in surrounding
areas. And the whole of the Yorkshire
force has been alerted. There is no
sign as yet of what motivated this
particularly brutal killing. This is Ken
Lewis I.R.N. Doncaster.

DAVID WILLIAMS: In the House of
Commons tonight, the Leader of the
Opposition, Margaret Thatcher
launched one of her most bitter attacks
yet on the Government in what is seen
as a further indication that an early
General Election is a possibility . . .

SECOND ANNOUNCER: A policeman
has been shot dead tonight in
Doncaster. His body was found in
Clive Road, by a deserted Cinema in
the Northern part of the city, he had
been shot several times.

THIRD ANNOUNCER: . . . was shot
dead tonight in Doncaster. He was a
young police constable out on his usual
beat. He was found lying outside a
deserted Cinema. He had been shot
four times at point blank range.

FOURTH ANNOUNCER: . . . in an
alleyway by a Cinema. His identity
has not as yet been released. Police
are anxious to talk to anyone who was
in, or near Clive Road between 9.30
and 10.30 tonight . . .

SECOND NEWSCAST
(Scene Seven)

Begins in blackout before the scene.
No fanfare. Half way through, it cuts to
the radio onstage as the lights come up.

DAVID WILLIAMS (*or perhaps another*
announcer): Following the shooting of
a Police Constable in Doncaster, police
are mounting a full scale manhunt,
North of Newcastle. Here is Ron Allen
in Newcastle.

RON ALLEN: After eye witness
accounts that two men and a woman,
thought to be in their twenties, were
seen leaving the area of the killing in a
van, Police here in Northumberland
are mounting one of the most massive
Manhunts ever seen in the North East.
Men have been drafted in from
surrounding forces and Scottish Police
have also been alerted. The three
young people are believed to be somewhere either in the hills in the Border
country, or just across the Border,
police are combing the lonely country
roads in that area and checking on
outlying farmhouses.
Helicopters are standing by for an
aerial search at sunrise. Police are
regarding the suspects as potentially
extremely dangerous, and both detec-
tives and many uniformed police have
been issued with firearms as they
attempt to encircle the whole area in
one large Police cordon.
This is Ron Allen I.R.N. Newcastle.